HOLY MASS

Approaches to the Mystery

NEW EDITION

by

A.-M. Roguet, O.P.

Translated

by

Matthew J. O'Connell

THE LITURGICAL PRESS
Collegeville, Minnesota

HOLY MASS — APPROACHES TO THE MYSTERY by Pere A.-M. Roguet, O.P., is the authorized English edition of *La messe — approches du mystère, Nouvelle* édition, published and copyrighted as number 9 in the *Livre de Vie* series by Éditions du Seuil, 27 rue Jacob, Paris, VI, France.

Nihil obstat: William G. Heidt, O.S.B., S.T.D., *Censor deputatus.* *Imprimatur:* ✠ George H. Speltz, D.D., Bishop of St. Cloud. St. Cloud, Minnesota, July 1, 1974.

Printed in the U.S.A. ISBN 0-8146-0297-5

Preface

This little book first appeared in 1951 (Éditions du Cerf) and was taken over unchanged into the *Livre de vie* series of Les Éditions du Seuil. In this form it acquired a large readership both in French and in various foreign languages.

After the Council, however, the liturgy of the Mass underwent profound changes. For this reason I wrote a new and different book, *Table ouverte ou la messe d'aujourd'hui* (Paris: Desclée, 2nd ed., 1970), in the form of a detailed commentary on the reformed rite.

The publishers of the *Livre de vie* series then asked me to consider updating the earlier book. I reread it with two concerns in mind. If it contained a large number of allusions to the old liturgy, would it not have to be completely redone? If so, would I not be forced to reproduce a large part of the text of my later book, to the point that the two books would really be the same?

My worries were in fact unfounded. Since the book dealt, not with the minute details of the liturgy, but with the essential structure of the Mass, I have been able to keep the overall framework of the first edition. In a number of ways, however, the book has been revised. To begin with, for biblical and liturgical citations I have used the official French text, which did not exist in 1951; at that time the whole Mass was said in Latin, while the translations in missals for the use of the faithful differed from one another.

Furthermore, I have had to add passages on new or reintroduced rites: the Prayer of the Faithful, concelebration, Communion from the chalice, the epiclesis. Most important of all, I have taken into account not only the Roman Canon but the "new" Eucharistic Prayers which can now replace it. Finally, I have eliminated many ideas that have now become useless, and I have entirely rewritten some passages.

I have kept the old title, *Holy Mass: Approaches to the Mystery*, because the purpose and basic structure remain the same. The book is still intended as an initiation in depth into the Mass — but the Mass in its present form. Such development within continuity is another proof, if proof still be needed, that the restored Mass is homogeneous in substance with the old Mass. It is always the sacrifice of Christ — the same yesterday, today, and forever — as well as the one, ever-old and ever-living sacrifice of the Church.

—A.-M. Roguet, O.P.

CONTENTS

HOLY MASS

Approaches to the Mystery

1.

The Assembly

THE MASS IS, BEFORE ALL ELSE, AN ASSEMBLY

We want to draw near to the mystery of the Mass. But since the Mass is a sign as well as a mystery, we must begin by looking at what is most immediately visible about the Mass, even to the eye of the unbeliever, and that is that the Mass is an assembly.

Here we have the outward feature which immediately describes our Mass. This characteristic was pointed out from the very beginning; the very first Christians "devoted themselves to the apostles' instruction and the communal life, to the breaking of bread and the prayers" (Acts 2:42). These various activities are to be understood, not as successive exercises, but as essential elements of the communal gatherings, with "the breaking of bread" designating our Mass. Further on in the same book, St. Luke writes: "On the first day of the week, when we *gathered* for the breaking of bread, Paul . . . kept on speaking until midnight" (Acts 20:7). Here we see the same elements of communal gathering, Eucharist, and preaching by the apostles.

When, around the year 55, St. Paul reproaches the Corinthians for their disorderly and uncharitable way of celebrating the Eucharist, he alludes again and again to the fact that people gathered together: "Your *meetings* are not profitable but harmful. First of all, I hear that when you *gather for a meeting* there are divisions among you. . . . When you *assemble* it is not to eat the Lord's Supper" (1 Cor. 11:17, 18, 20); in practice you deny the Eucharist as the sacrament of unity. "Therefore, my brothers, when you *assemble* for the meal, wait for one another. . . . so that your *assembly* may not deserve condemnation" (1 Cor. 11:33-34).

Around A.D. 111-113, Pliny the Younger sent Emperor Trajan a report on what he had been able to find out about the life-style of Christians. He noted that "they are accustomed to *gather* on a set day, before dawn."

Around A.D. 150, St. Justin began his description of the Mass with these words: "On the day dedicated to the sun,[1] all who live in the towns or countryside *gather in one place.*" He had earlier ended his description of baptism by writing that "after having baptized in this way the person who believes and comes to us, we bring him to the brothers (as we call them) where they have *gathered together*" for the celebration of Mass.

THE MYSTERY OF THE CHURCH

This "gathering together" is something more than practical necessity. It is itself already a mystery, and an essential one at that — the very mystery of the Church. The Greek word for "church," *ekklēsia*, means "a gathering," and referred to the assembly of the faithful before it came to be applied to the place where the assembly was held. The very place itself, then, as the name given to it indicates, is more than a simple locale; it becomes the sacrament and parable of the mystery which is the Christian assembly. The stones that are brought together, "built" together, do more than just shelter the gathering; they signify, in the building they compose, the inexpressible mystery of the "living stones" which make up the "edifice of spirit" (1 Peter 2:5), the "holy temple in the Lord," the "dwelling place for God," which rises on the foundation of the apostles and prophets, with Christ Jesus himself as the capstone" (Eph. 2:20-22).

In destroying the sin which had torn apart the peoples of the earth, Christ had no other purpose than "to gather into one all the dispersed children of God" (John 11:52). When thus gathered, not by chance or necessity but in order to worship, Christians are the Body of Christ; as soon as they are gathered, Christ is there present, even before the consecration of the bread and wine into his body and blood.[2]

"THE LORD . . . WITH YOU"

This is the reason for the greeting which the celebrant gives the assembly at various points in the Mass: *Dominus vobiscum.* The usual translation is "The Lord be with you"; the origin of the phrase, if this translation given in some very popular Bibles is accepted, is found in Boaz's greeting to the harvesters (Ruth 2:4). Attention is also called to the greeting of the risen Christ to his apostles: *Pax vobis* (John 20:19, 21, 26; Luke 24:36), which in the liturgy is reserved to the bishop, because he is, beyond all others, Christ's representative in the Church. And as *Pax vobis* is translated "Peace be with you," so *Dominus vobiscum* likewise is accorded the optative form "The Lord be with you."

But *Pax vobis* could just as well be translated "Peace *is* with you," since the words are spoken by

Christ as he appears in the midst of the gathered apostles, and he "*is* our peace" (Eph. 2:14). Moreover, *Dominus vobiscum* need not be derived from modern versions of Boaz's greeting to the harvesters. An angel addresses Gideon: "The Lord *is* with you, O champion!" (Judg. 6:12). Most importantly, another angel comes to Mary and says to her: *Dominus tecum,* which we correctly translate: "The Lord is with you" (Luke 1:28). Why, then, should we not take the same greeting, now cast in the plural, as meaning: "The Lord *is* with you"? Did not Jesus himself say: "Where two or three are gathered in my name, *there am I* in their midst" (Matthew 18:20)?

Herein lies the mystery of the Christian assembly: an invisible but real[3] presence of Christ (though not a "substantial" presence such as is effected in the Eucharistic consecration) in the midst of those who are gathered "in his name," that is, in order to pray "through him, with him, and in him." Bossuet put it very well: "The Church is Jesus Christ, but Jesus Christ diffused and communicated." Where the Church is, Jesus is. Such an assembly therefore merits respect and devotion; it deserves that we greet it as rendering Christ himself present. It is precisely because Jesus is in their midst that Christians form " 'a chosen race, a royal priesthood, a holy nation, a people he [God] claims for his own,'" or again, a "holy priesthood" (1 Peter 2:9, 5).

THE MYSTERY OF THE ASSEMBLY, AN EFFECT OF BAPTISM

We are not to believe, however, that the Christian assembly is holy and renders Christ present simply because men have come together; individual sinners would in that case become divinized simply because they unite into a group. That would be to cultivate a mob mystique, a romantic democratism after the fashion of Victor Hugo or Jules Michelet which cannot be squared with Catholic doctrine. If these people form a "holy priesthood," it is basically because they have been baptized. Baptism has not only cleansed them individually from original sin and bestowed the gift of grace upon them; it has also brought them to rebirth as the "people of God," as "a people he claims for his own." He makes of them "living stones" which are part of "God's house."

If the parish Mass, which is the authentic, official "common gathering," is preceded by the misunderstood and neglected ceremony of blessing and sprinkling water, it is in order to express the fact that the waters of baptism (now recalled by the blessed water) have gathered these people into a Church which can offer to the Father the sacrifice of Christ.

There is another vestige, even less visible, of this link between baptism and the Mass. It is the custom, still alive in some provinces and surviving everywhere (in France) at funeral services, of grouping men and women separately on the two sides of the church. In antiquity, baptism was really a bath (that is the meaning of the word "baptism") and required nudity. Consequently it was administered separately to men and women, who were accompanied by godfathers or godmothers respectively; the function of the latter was to undress the candidates, help them down into and up out of the baptismal pool, dry them off, and reclothe them. The newly baptized, with candles in their hands, then entered the church in two lines, the men on one side, the women on the other; here, for the first time, they were to take part in the entire Mass with the community. (The First Communion procession has retained several elements of the ancient procession of the newly baptized.) During the Easter Vigil, the early Christians sang the *Vidi aquam;* this can still be sung throughout the paschal season for the sprinkling of water before Mass to remind us that if "the Lord is with us," it is because of our baptism.

HIERARCHIC ORDERING OF THE ASSEMBLY

The Christian assembly at Mass, which has been brought into being through a new and supernatural birth, is also a hierarchic assembly. It is not an amorphous collection but an organized body. The body has a head, a leader. Not only does it have an invisible Head, Christ, but also a visible head, the priest. He too brings about the presence of Christ, but in a new way. That is why in answer to his *Dominus vobiscum,* the assembly answers with an equivalent greeting: *Et cum spiritu tuo,* "The Lord be with your spirit." The meaning of this is not simply "The Lord be with you too," but "May the Lord communicate his Spirit to your spirit for the sacred function you are about to undertake."

The priest is indeed incorporated into Christ through baptism so as to form, in union with all his brothers — each in his place and all together — the Body of Christ. But beyond this, through ordination he receives the power, proper to himself, to take the place of Christ, to speak and act in his name, to lend him his mouth and hands in order to say and do again what Christ said and did at the Last Supper. So true is this that he can say, in all truth, "This is *my* body." The priest is not satisfied simply to quote the words of Christ; he makes them his own and is, at this moment, in a sacramental fashion, Christ himself. Otherwise anyone at all, even a pagan, could consecrate the Eucharist by quoting Christ's words.

Since Christ is Head of his Church, since he contains the Church and sums it up in himself, the priest who is ordained to take Christ's place represents, by that very fact, the whole assembly. Not only does he speak to, greet, and exhort the faithful, but he also speaks to God in their name. He is not the deputy of the faithful, his power does not come from them, but he represents them as he does Christ.[4] This is why throughout the Mass (except in devotional prayers which conern the priest alone and are said in a low voice) he always expresses himself in the plural. For when he prays, he is only the mouthpiece of the assembly.

For clearer grasp of the hierarchic organization of the assembly, we must also take note of the intermediary officers who link the assembly with the priest. We are referring to the various ministers. They do not exempt the assembly from answering and taking part, but carry out various functions in its name (deacon, acolyte), or are delegated by the principal celebrant to proclaim the word of God to the assembly (deacon, readers), or maintain order in the assembly and guide its movements so that it may act as an organized living body (for example, the action of welcoming, which corresponds to what was done by the old order of "porters"). Finally, the choir is not primarily a body of professional singers but a delegation of the assembly, an elite group commissioned to lead the communal singing or to perform for the assembly the more difficult chants, which are meant to nourish the meditative reflection of the assembly and to enable it to share in the praise of God in silent, attentive wonder. For this reason the choir should take a place in front of the nave, linking it to the altar.

Since Christ is the cornerstone of the Church, the altar, which represents him, is the most sacred place in the building and the center of attention for the assembly. In former times, and more and more consciously today, the assembly gathers around the altar. The memento of the living in the Latin Roman Canon calls the faithful the *circumstantes:* those who are *around* the altar, and *standing,* as active participants, men awake and risen.

One of the things that shows the unity of an assembly, its vitality, and its participation in the action taking place at the altar is its uniformity in posture and, among various postures, the frequent standing position. To an eye not blinded by routine, there is no more disheartening spectacle than those disorganized Christian assemblies in which some are kneeling in a posture of private prayer, while others are standing in a posture of active sharing or of indifference, and still others are sitting without showing much awareness of why they do so. (In itself the posture of kneeling or sitting is a very worthy one, suited for contrite prayer or for listening and meditation.)

Nor is anything more distressing than the anarchic arrangement of those gatherings that leave wide empty spaces around the altar, while the area near the holy water fonts and the doors are mobbed with people who seem to want to remain apart, not to get involved with the community, and to remain as far removed as possible from what is going on at the distant altar.

It may be argued that these deplorable discrepancies within the assembly are due chiefly to the large number of people who come late. True enough. But is not this vary tardiness a sign that people do not respect the assembly and are more concerned to fulfill an individual obligation (the manner does not matter) than to enter into the inner mystery of the praying assembly?

In the early Church, care was taken to arrange, from the very beginning of Mass, an ordered grouping of the people present. The "porters" saw to this, as welcoming ushers often do today where the clergy cannot be spared for the function. Often, too, the assembly of old became aware of its unity through the custom of the "station," of which our complete missals kept some indication until recently. There were not the great number of Masses that we have today, for with the huge growth in the number of Catholics, multiple Masses is the only reasonable, pastoral response. When there were only a few Catholics in a given area, only one Mass in a church was sufficient. If there happened to be several bishops or priests present, they stood around the principal celebrant and concelebrated with him.

On more important days there was also a "station"; the whole clergy and people of the city gathered at one church (the term "station" derives from a military term meaning a troop under arms and on the alert). To give the gathering an even greater visibility, the people first assembled in another church, the church of the *collecta*, i.e., of assembly or gathering. At this spot the porters assigned people their places, and all went in procession to the station church, singing the Litany of the Saints, a popular prayer to which everyone could respond; thus the people provided others and themselves with the stirring and meaningful sight of an organized and unified assembly, a Church on the pilgrimage journey to heaven. Mass could now begin and the celebrant could greet this congregation of the baptized with *Dominus vobiscum*. "The Lord is with you," brothers, because you are his Body. But also: "May the Lord be with you," for the action we are to celebrate together will make him even more present by uniting you more fully, through the mystery of the same offering and sacrifice and the one meal, to the Body which you already are.

CONCELEBRATION

The Second Vatican Council has restored to the Latin Church a rite which helps us to enter more fully into the mystery of the assembly: *concelebration*, the rite of a Mass which, instead of being presided over by one priest, involves several celebrants. This does not mean that all do the same actions and say the same prayers, as in the practice of what were called for a while "synchronized Masses." In concelebration there is only one Mass, and the several priests play different parts in it. The principal concelebrant presides over the whole assembly and says the prayers proper to him in this role; the other priests perform various secondary functions, such as proclaiming the readings, leading the intercessory prayers, and distributing Communion. All, however, recite together that which is the heart of the Eucharistic prayer: the petition for consecration, the consecration of the bread and wine, the prayer of remembrance which follows the consecration, and the conclusion: "Through him, with him, in him. . . ."

All this concerns only the priests. But concelebration also shows the faithful that though the individual priest has the power to consecrate, he is also part of a *presbyterium,* or collective, communal priestly body. The unity in diversity which is characteristic of the Church can find its model and source in this sharing of many priests, with their diverse apostolic activities, in one and the same Eucharistic action. The faithful thus find the mystery of the assembly brought home to them through the vital action at which they are present and in which they share (for they too "concelebrate" in their own way and in accordance with their place in the Church).

This is why concelebration is required on those occasions when the priesthood is to be shown as a unified body at the service of the one Church. Thus, we have concelebration at the ordination of a priest or the consecration of a bishop, that is, at the rite which incorporates them into the presbyteral or episcopal college; at the consecration of the holy oils by the bishop in his cathedral on Holy Thursday; and finally on Holy Thursday evening, in all parishes with several priests, at the commemoration of the institution of the Eucharist by Christ, the one Priest, in the midst of his apostles.

From another viewpoint, even in these few years since its introduction, the practice of concelebration has already worked against the unity which it should foster. Especially in the United States, where the practice of participating in Sunday Mass had always rated a phenomenally high percentage, an increasing number of parish groups are now being denied the advantage of a sufficient number of Mass services to accommodate the crowds seeking unity with Christ through the Eucharistice sacrifice. No longer are priests eager to leave their religious houses or clerical centers to assist at mission churches or parishes with thousands of parishioners. It is a false application of the principle of concelebration to refuse to supply the spiritual needs of others and justifying such action on the basis of displaying the "unity of the presbyterium."

[1]Justin uses the idiom of the pagans to whom he is addressing his *Apology*. The name "day of the sun" survives in the English *Sunday* and the German *Sonntag* (Dutch: *Zondag*). Christians, on the other hand, were already speaking of "the Lord's day," *dominica dies*, from which the modern Romance languages derive their word for the first day of the week (French: *dimanche;* Italian: *domenica;* Spanish and Portuguese: *domingo*).

[2]Cf. Vatican II, *Constitution on the Sacred Liturgy*, no. 7, in Walter M. Abbott (ed.), *The Documents of Vatican II* (New York: Herder and Herder, Association Press, 1966), pp. 140-141.

[3]Cf. Pope Paul VI, *Mysterium Fidei: On the Doctrine and Worship of the Holy Eucharist*, September 3, 1965, in *The Pope Speaks*, 10 (1964-65), pp. 309-329; Sacred Congregation of Rites, *Eucharisticum Mysterium: On the Worship of the Eucharistic Mystery*, May 25, 1967, no. 9, in *The Pope Speaks*, 12 (1967), p. 217.

[4]Cf. Vatican II, *Dogmatic Constitution on the Church*, no. 10; Abbott, pp. 26-27.

2.

The Sacrifice of Praise

THE IMPORTANCE OF SINGING IN THE MASS

Another characteristic of the Catholic Mass liturgy is song. Past history with its share of abuse in matters of music or the dislike of certain people for singing may have occasioned the idea that singing is something decorative but accidental in the liturgy. But singing is, in fact, essential. A celebration without song will always be abnormal and, as it were, stunted, and should therefore be the exception, not the rule.

To begin with, singing is a sign of collective prayer. The separate voices unite and become one in song. Moreover, the singing of the acclamations reserved for the congregation makes it possible for them to unite with the priest in unanimity of intention. Furthermore, singing manifests joy and praise. The Mass is a festival, a "sacrifice of praise." This last expression comes from Psalm 50, which is an invitation to worship in spirit and in truth: "Offer God praise as your sacrifice and fulfill your vows to the Most High" (v. 14). At the end of same psalm, God is still speaking and says: "He that offers praise as a sacrifice glorifies me; and to him that goes the right way I will show the salvation of God" (v. 23). The phrase is also found in Psalm 116, which is intended

13

for use in a thanksgiving sacrifice for deliverance from a great trial (to which Psalm 115 refers): "What return shall I make to the Lord for all that he has given me? I will take the cup of salvation and call upon the name of the Lord. I will fulfill my vows to the Lord, in the presence of all his people . . . Lord, . . . I will offer you a *sacrifice of praise*" (vv. 12-14, 17).

THE MASS; A SACRIFICE OF PRAISE

The same expression is used as a name for the Mass, and this at the very heart of the Mass, in the remembrance of the living (Roman Canon): "We offer you this *sacrifice of praise*. . . ." This does not, of course, prevent the Mass from being at the same time a sacrifice of expiation and propitiation, for the prayer continues: "for ourselves and those who are dear to us. We pray to you, our living and true God, for our well-being and redemption."

The Council of Trent, in fact, forbade reducing the Mass to a sacrifice of praise pure and simple: "If anyone says that the Sacrifice of the Mass is merely an offering of praise and of thanksgiving, . . . and not propitiatory . . . let him be anathema."[1] But this does not preclude us from affirming that the Mass is *also* a sacrifice of praise.

THE CROSS AND PRAISE

On first hearing, the above may surprise us. Is not the Mass the re-presentation of the Cross? Of course it is. But the Cross itself is not simply and solely a redemptive sacrifice. Or better, we must give "redemption" its full and positive significance. Redemption is not only the destruction of sin; such a destruction is indeed necessary as a means, as the removal of an obstacle, but it is not the ultimate purpose of the sacrifice.

God created man solely for his own glory, that is, he intended men to praise him, to know him, but with the wonder that transforms simple knowledge into praise. He intended man to make all creation, even the parts of it that are not endowed with knowledge, sing the praise of its Lord: "Bless the Lord, all you works of the Lord, praise and exalt him above all forever" (Dan. 3:57).[2]

Sin is a stigma that prevents man from mirroring the glory of God. Sin detracts from God's glory, not only because it is an offense against the rights of God but also because it tarnishes the mirror in which God's glory ought to shine forth in the form of praise. Redemption gets rid of sin. But to what purpose, if not to reconcile men with the Father and to give them access to him? Redemption does, of course, re-establish the rights of God that have been offended by sin, but it also aims to let man celebrate the glory of God.

The Cross, then, though an instrument of torment, is also and above all a trophy of victory. It brings into being the new people of God, which has the duty and the ability, far more than the first people of God, to sing his praise and to proclaim his "wonderful deeds."[3] St. Thomas Aquinas, in his treatise on the sacraments, makes the profound observation that Christ "by his Passion inaugurated the cultic economy of the Christian religion."[4] To this we may link the statement, frequently found in the Fathers, that the Church (the society founded by Jesus unto the praise of God) is born of water (symbol of baptism) and blood (symbol of the Mass) which flowed from the opened side of the Crucified.

In light of this, we can also understand the surprising epithet "blessed" that is applied to the Passion in the prayer of remembrance, or anamnesis, which always follows immediately upon the consecration in the official Roman Canon. The Passion was painful indeed but also blessed, that is, beatifying and glorious, since it glorified God by bringing into existence the choir of the redeemed who sing the glory of the Lamb that was slain yet lives. We are alluding, of course, to the Apocalypse, which is filled with hymns of praise and which describes heaven as a glorious liturgy.

The Mass re-presents the Cross, but it does so by renewing the Supper which relates to, contains, and signifies the Cross. Now the Supper was a sacrifice celebrated in the form of a meal, that is, of a joyous action that takes place in a festive atmosphere. Jesus wanted a spacious and well-furnished room (Luke 22:12; Mark 14:15); we may assume that the meal was a good one. Jesus consecrated his body and blood in a "eucharist," that is, a prayer of praise and thanksgiving addressed to his Father.

But did not the presence of Judas and the imminence of the Passion cast a shadow on the occasion? Undoubtedly. But if we read the Gospels carefully, we will be persuaded that Jesus was in a hurry to send Judas away; his sinister presence poisoned the sweet joy of that supreme moment.[5] Finally, when the meal was over, Matthew 26:30 and Mark 14:26 tell us, those present sang the psalms of the *Hallel*, that is, the thanksgiving Psalms 113-118, which therefore include Psalm 116 (the "sacrifice of praise") and the little psalm of triumph, 117 ("Praise the Lord, all you nations"), which is often sung after Benediction of the Blessed Sacrament.

Since it re-presents the Cross according to the rite of the Supper, our Mass has all the characteristics of the Supper, and is made even more joyful by the fact that it is no longer overshadowed by the approach of the Passion. We may note, finally, that in the minds of the apostles, the Mass recalled not only the Supper — the meal beyond all others — but all the meals taken by Jesus, especially the very joyous ones that followed upon his resurrection. In one of his sermons, St. Peter makes the revealing and touching remark: "They killed him . . . only to have God raise him up on the third day and grant that he be seen, not by all, but only by such witnesses as had been chosen beforehand by God — *by us who ate and drank with him after he rose from the dead*" (Acts 10:40-41).

PRAISE IN THE MASS

We have been explaining why the Mass is a sacrifice of praise. We must now see in what ways this is so. The real beginning of the Mass is marked by the singing of the Entrance Song. Most of the time this song is taken from the psalms, or at least it is sung together with a psalm; another song may be substituted for the psalm. Later comes *the* psalm of the Mass — the one between the first two Readings. It is always possible to find among the psalms one that will be appropriate for any feast in the liturgical cycle. The reason is, as Dionysius the Areopagite remarks, that "the psalms contain, in the form of praise, everything to be found in Sacred Scripture." The Prologue of St. Augustine's *Commentary on the Psalms* is even more explicit:

> The Psalter is a universal treasure-house of good teaching and furnishes each reader with what he

needs. . . . And it does it melodiously and to the sound of delightful singing. . . . The psalms bring harmony to those who are divided and reconciles enemies. For how can you go on calling a man your enemy when you join in singing the same psalm to God? . . . . They provide beginners with the rudiments, those progressing with growth, and the perfect with unyielding strength, being as they are *the single voice of the whole Church.* The psalms embellish our solemnities. . . . They are the occupation of the angles and the spiritual incense offered by the heavenly host.[6]

St. Paul urges the Colossians to devote themselves to praising God: "Let the word of Christ, rich as it is, dwell in you. In wisdom made perfect, instruct and admonish one another. Sing gratefully to God from your hearts in psalms, hymns, and inspired songs" (Col. 3:16). What is left of these "hymns" and "inspired songs" (or "spiritual canticles") which Paul mentions alongside the psalms? We may perhaps detect some traces of them in Paul's own writings (cf., e.g., Phil. 2:6-11; Eph. 5:14). Our "Glory to God in the highest" is probably one of them; it may even be the hymn which, according to Pliny's testimony, the Christians "sang to Christ as to a god." Before becoming part of the Mass, the *Gloria* was sung in the Office, like our *Te Deum,* another "spiritual canticle." Both are songs of praise which do not come from Sacred Scripture, but which sprang in lyric and freely rhythmed form from the hearts of the early Christians.

Our Liturgy of the Word contains further elements which make it a "sacrifice of praise," even if we do not usually think of them in this light. First of all, there is the Collect (sometimes called: Opening Prayer) and the other prayers. The body of the prayer consists of a variable request, but the request is introduced by an exclamation of praise, a reminder of the divine attributes: "Almighty and eternal God"; "Almighty and merciful God"; "Lord God, you show your power above all through mercy and forgiveness"; "Lord God, your foreknowledge is never proved wrong as you carry out your plans"; "Lord God, our refuge and our strength." Above all, however, no Roman Collect ends without a doxology, or formula of praise, that is wide-ranging and solemn in tone: "Through our Lord Jesus Christ, your Son, who lives and reigns with you and the Holy Spirit, one God, for ever and ever."

Such a prayer-structure teaches us two very important lessons. First, if prayer is to be heard, it must begin and end with praise. Second, the doxology shows us the normal course or "economy" to be followed in Christian praise. The praise is addressed *to* the Father; it is presented to him *by* or through the mediator and ambassador of praise who is the Son; it is uttered *in* the life-giving and unifying might of the Holy Spirit, the soul of the Church. This economy characterizes the whole Mass, as may readily be seen by examining most of the Prefaces, which initiate the central, consecratory part of the sacrifice, and the great doxology which concludes it.

THE PRAISE VALUE OF THE READINGS

What we may find even more surprising is that the Readings, too, contribute to make the Liturgy of the Word a sacrifice of praise. It is true, of course, that the purpose of the Readings is to instruct the faithful; did not this first part of the Mass used to be called the "Mass of the Catechumens," that is, of those who were receiving instruction with a view to baptism? Nonetheless, this was no ordinary instruction. For the word of God does not have instruction alone as its purpose; or, more accurately, when it instructs, it does so not simply to enlighten the mind but to reveal the great deeds of God and to stir man to praise. The word of God is therefore not simply spoken aloud — it is proclaimed. A Preface for the feasts of the Blessed Virgin does more than bid us give thanks; it urges us to "praise, bless, and proclaim" (in the official Church Sacramentary). The three verbs are almost synonymous, inasmuch as "to proclaim" *(praedicare)* is not simply to enunciate or establish truths, but also to praise and bless, that is, to shout aloud and exalt the greet deeds of God. God alone can praise himself worthily, and he does so through his word. If so many christians lack the spirit of praise, it is because they are unfamiliar with God's word; they do not know how either to receive it or to utter it back to God.

Finally, the Creed, by which we reply to God's word and express our adherence to it, is not a simple doctrinal summary. When proclaimed by the assembly of the baptized, it is a profession of faith and a "confession," or joyful acknowledgment, of God's great deeds.

We would, then, distort the true nature of the Mass if we saw in its first part only a didactic introduction to the sacrifice. Admittedly, Readings are meant to be understood. But the intelligibility in question here is not simply a rational one; the aim is rather to enter into the mystery and the sacrifice of praise. Such penetration calls for more than intellectual docility, such as is required by a catechism lesson; it requires a lyrical attention, a sharing of enthusiasm.

As a matter of fact, the whole Mass is a sacrifice of praise. As we shall see, the sacrifice, strictly so called, of the Body of Christ takes the form of a "eucharist," or thanksgiving. Thanksgiving, however, is but the crowning perfection of praise. The Liturgy of the Word involves us deeply in the sacrifice of praise; its variety teaches us to vary and adapt our praise according to the season or feast. The habitual latecomer and the person who is inattentive and neglects to participate in the Liturgy of the Word share only in an improverished, monotonous way in the Eucharistic sacrifice itself. There is no question but that history, rubrics, and casuistry authorize a distinction between two major parts of the Mass. But in reality the entire Mass is a sacrifice of praise. Thus the Eucharistic sacrifice in the more limited sense is already determined and colored by the Liturgy of the Word.

IS PRAISE A SACRIFICE?

What has been said helps us understand that the expression "sacrifice of praise" is not a metaphor. You may ask: What sacrifice or immolation is there in a series of songs and readings? We will see later on that sacrifice does not necessarily involve a bloody immolation. Sacrifice is rather a sacred, sanctifying action, and the sharing in song, the work of praising God, the fervent reception of God's word are already consecrating and sanctifying. They prepare and perfect the people of God for the sacrifice.

But for the sake of argument, let us accept the usual meaning given to the word "sacrifice." The person who forgets himself in song, surrenders his own narrow concerns in order to sing the glory of

God, and lets himself be penetrated to the heart and transformed by God's word is surely undergoing, is he not, a purifying, self-stripping action that might well be called an immolation, even though it be done with joy? That is perhaps the ultimate reason why so many Christians shy away from song and praise — behind their appeal to dignity and recollection is a lack of the self-forgetful simplicity that a genuine sacrifice requires.

---

[1]Henry Denzinger, *Enchiridion symbolorum, definitionum, et declarationum de rebus fidei et morum*, 32nd ed. by Adolf Schönmetzer (Freiburg: Herder, 1963), no. 1753; older editions, (*D*), no. 750. Translated in *The Church Teaches: Documents of the Church in English Translation*, selected and translated by John F. Clarkson, S. J., *et al.* (St. Louis: B. Herder Book Co., 1955), no. 758, p. 295.

[2]The text is from the Song of the Three Young Men in the Fiery Furnace, which is used at Lauds on Sunday.

[3]This expression recurs frequently in the psalms; cf. Pss. 26:7; 78:4, 11, 12, 32; 105:2, 5; 106:7, 22; 107:8, 15, 21, 24, 31; 111:4.

[4]*Summa theologiae*, III, q. 62, a. 5.

[5]Exegetes today agree that Judas left the supper room before the institution of the Eucharist.

[6]The Prologue is, in fact, the work of St. Basil; it can be found in *PL* 36:63–66.

3.

The Eucharist

The Liturgy of the Word is continued by, and fulfilled in, the Eucharistic liturgy. Our first task is to come to grips with the meaning of the term "eucharist."

The early Christians generally used other names: the breaking of bread, the Lord's supper, the assembly; we shall come back to these later. Modern Christians usually speak of Mass, Communion, the Blessed Sacrament. But the official term, and the one the catechisms use in enumerating the seven sacraments, is Eucharist. The word is of Greek origin, which makes it sound a bit pedantic. Yet it was not the theologians who coined it, for it comes directly from the Gospel. It derives from the verb *eucharistein*, which means "to give thanks."[1]

Thus we see Jesus giving thanks to his Father at the moment of raising Lazarus (John 11:41) and at the moment of the miraculous multiplication of loaves, which prefigured the Eucharist (John 6:11). Above all, he gave thanks to his Father on Holy Thursday as he gave his disciples the bread that was now his body (Luke 22:19; 1 Cor. 11:24), and the cup of his blood, the Eucharistic cup (Matthew 26:27; Mark 14:23).

Before multiplying the loaves (Matthew 14:19; Mark 6:41; Luke 9:16) and before breaking bread for the disciples as Emmaus (Luke 24:30), he "blessed his Father"; under a different verb, the same kind of prayer of thanksgiving seems to be meant.[2] But it is the word "eucharist" or "thanksgiving" that has characterized the sacrament of bread and cup, of the body and blood of Jesus given as food and drink.

In thus thanking God, Jesus was simply conforming to a religious custom of the Jews. For, whether a meal was a Passover meal or simply that of a group of friends, the father of the family pronounced a thanksgiving or blessing addressed to God, thanking him for his major benefactions: the creation of the world; the gift of food to men; the calling and liberation of the Chosen People at the first Passover when they escaped from Egyptian enslavement and the kingdom of idols, crossed the Red Sea, and entered the promised land.

THE IMPORTANCE OF THE PREFACE

Such a rite was not accidental or secondary. In her Mass liturgy the Church has kept this thanksgiving and given it central importance. It marks the beginning of the great consecratory action, initiated by what we call the Preface. The latter is not a simple prelude or prologue, as the term "preface" might suggest; it is rather a solemn proclamation of God's saving deeds and stirs us to vital participation in the sacrifice.

The celebrant invites the faithful to raise their hearts to God, then to offer thanks: "Let us give thanks to the Lord our God." When the people answer: "It is right to give him thanks and praise," he takes up that motif and develops it: "Father, all-powerful and ever-living God, we do well always and everywhere to give you thanks through Jesus Christ our Lord." He goes on to point out the motives for such thanksgiving, often drawing them from the mystery expressed in the feast or season, and concludes by saying that in this thanksgiving we join the countless multitude of angels in heaven, who sing unceasingly: "Holy, holy, holy!" The Mass, which enters into its essential phase with the Preface, is essentially an act of thanksgiving.

WHAT IS THANKSGIVING?

What precisely is an act of thanksgiving? What does the expression "to give thanks" mean? As a matter of fact, we hardly ever come across the phrase except as part of our Christian vocabulary. This does not mean that the expression is outmoded and ought to be replaced by a more contemporary one. Some people, in the interests of adaptation, would like to substitute "acclaim" or "congratulate." Such substitutions would be a betrayal of the idea. The fact that we cannot find a synonym for "thank" simply shows that the word expresses a profoundly religious idea which has no parallel in ordinary life.

God created all things. All that we have, all that we are, we owe to his goodness, and the most basic response of a religious soul is to acknowledge the debt. Everything has been given to us, and therefore we have nothing to give in return. We cannot pay God back, any more than a child can repay or reward his parents for the gift of life, nourishment, education, and, above all, love. But he does not therefore have the right to be ungrateful. He must recognize all that he owes to them and that his debt can never be repaid. All they ask of him is that he acknowledge the debt, and acknowledge it with love. That is what thanksgiving is. It is the opposite of ingratitude; it is not a payment but the acknowledgment of our all-embracing debt to God, an acknowledgment that is accompanied by enthusiasm, love, and adoration. A "thank you" for an ordinary, everyday act of courtesy is adequate payment, but the thanksgiving of which we are speaking here never comes to its end.

This short description allows us to suggest some elements that go into thanksgiving. We say merely "suggest" and "some elements," for thanksgiving is something so comprehensive, so complex, and yet so simple, that there is no truly adequate definition of it. To thank, then, is to acknowledge that we owe everything to God. It means to acknowledge both the greatness of God, our sole Creator and Benefactor, and our own nothingness. For we have nothing and can give nothing that we have not first received.

In giving thanks, we assert simultaneously that we cannot pay our debt and that we are deeply aware of this unpayable debt. If thanksgiving, in this sense, were addressed to a fellow creature, however superior to us he might be, it would be humiliating and distressing. But since it is directed to God, we can find joy in acknowledging not only the gift but our inability to repay it. Thanksgiving, far from humiliating us or rousing resentment in us, is made up of joy, affection, admiration, enthusiasm, along with gratitude and humility. Far fram abasing us, it increases our stature; far from saddening us, it fills us with joy.

Thanksgiving is an unlimited and inexhaustible sentiment, for it encompasses everything. It embraces the rich beauty of the visible world; this is why the sight of a beautiful landscape, a sunrise, a growing plant, a sleeping child, makes us feel the need to give thanks. Thanksgiving also embraces invisible wonders: the beauty of the human soul, the inner riches of the saints, the fruitfulness of the sacraments, the sweetness of God's word, the greatness of the Church, Finally — and here it acquires its purest form — thanksgiving embraces God himself: his goodness, his greatness, his eternal happiness — in a word, his glory. In the hymn *"Glory to God in the highest,"* we utter the sublime acclamation; "We give you thanks, we praise you for your glory."

Thanksgiving is the purest, noblest, and most exalted of sentiments, because it is the most disinterested one that can inspire a devout soul. Unfortunately it is not the most natural nor the most frequent. How many persons who regard themselves as "good Christians" spend their time in self-pity and petitions to God for material or spiritual benefits! It is true that Christ told us: "Ask and you shall receive" and that petition is an integral part of prayer. But St. Paul, with great psychological insight, was able, to combine the two elements: "Dismiss all anxiety from your minds. Present your needs to God in every form of prayer and in petitions full of gratitude" (Phil. 4:6). Thus, to unite thanksgiving to petition is a good way of being heard, for you show your benefactor that you are not ungrateful.

We are accustomed to think of the sacraments as God's gifts to us in our wretched condition and as answers to our needs. But is not man's noblest need the need to be grateful? The Eucharist is not only the sacrament which gives us Christ's body as food; it is also, and even primarily, the sacrament which allows us to express thanks to God.

In the Eucharist, however, our thanksgiving does not remain simply a sentiment; rather, it takes form in bread and wine. These we can offer to God because they are the work of our hands; at the same time they can express our gratitude, because we could never have produced bread and wine if God had not first given us earth and sky, sun and rain, kernels and grapes.

After the consecration we will address the Father: "from the many gifts you have given us we offer to you. . . ." The Eastern liturgies use an even stronger expression: we offer you "what is yours from what is yours."

CHRIST IS HIMSELF A THANKSGIVING

If we were able to offer God nothing but bread and wine, that is, a very small bit of his creation, our thanksgiving would certainly be ridiculously inadequate, inasmuch as all we have is from him. But the sacrifice of the Mass makes it possible for us to offer God a thanksgiving which is fully worthy of him. The reason is that the bread and wine will become the very Person of his Son. He is the great Singer of God, the only one who can offer God a perfect thanksgiving that is far more than a matter of words and feelings. He is not satisfied to take our thanksgiving and present it to the Father. No, he *is* himself a thanksgiving. Being truly man, a creature like ourselves, he knows our nothingness, shares our wretchedness, and is aware of our powerlessness. Being God from God, truly Son of God and Word of the Father, he has perfect knowledge of the Father's glory and reflects this glory in a perfect way (cf. Heb. 1:3). As Man-God, he is the first-born of all mankind and sums up all creation; inasmuch as his whole being is a movement of "going to the Father" and he is "the way" to the Father, he brings all creation and all mankind back to the Father.

This, then, is why our Mass is a perfect act of thanksgiving: it offers the Father not only our songs and acclamations, and not only bread and wine, but also the very Person of Christ, in whom "we can speak freely to God, drawing near him with confidence" (Eph. 3:12). For "he is the image of the invisible God, the first-born of all creatures. In him everything in heaven and on earth was created . . .; all were created through him, and for him. . . . It pleased God to make absolute fullness reside in him and, by means of him, to reconcile everything in his person" (Col. 1:15-20).

All this is brought out quite clearly in the two prayers which conclude the Canon. The priest says first: "Through Christ our Lord you give us all these gifts. You fill them with life and goodness, you bless them and make them holy." Thus all creation is related to the Father through Christ, the Head of creation. Then the priest elevates the chalice and the paten bearing the consecrated bread, and concludes: "Through him, with him, in him, in the unity of the Holy Spirit, all glory and honor is yours, almighty Father, for ever and ever."

THE AMEN

The response of the faithful to this great doxology[3] is "Amen." This Amen is the high point of their expression of participation in the thanksgiving and praise given to God through the Eucharistic sacrifice. St. Jerome tells us that at Rome in his day the Amen echoed like thunder. Today this Amen of the

faithful is a timid thing (if they bother to say it at all).
Is this not, in part at least, because the meaning of it
escapes them? This in turn is due to the false
translation which has long been in use and which
suggests, not enthusiastic affirmation, but passive
resignation: "So be it." (The fault can ultimately be
laid at the door of the Seventy who translated the Old
Testament into Greek. The Latin translation, the
Vulgate, kept the word Amen.)

Amen does not mean "So be it." When Jesus
begins a statement with "Amen," we do not translate
this as "So be it," but as "Truly." So, too, the Amen
which ends the sign of the Cross or the Creed is not
the answer to some wish that has been expressed but a
concluding affirmation. Frenchmen prior to the
Revolution still said, for example at the beginning of a
notarized document, "In the name of the Father and of
the Son and of the Holy Spirit. Amen." Amen is
equivalent to saying: "This is true," but with
overtones of enthusiasm. It is a word expressive of
faith, thanksgiving, and praise, and, all in all, it would
be better to leave it untranslated. It is Hebrew in
origin and is connected with a root word meaning
solidity and confidence. Isaias, for example, says that
our God is an "Amen God" (65:16). The word has
passed untranslated into all languages.

It is true that "Amen" is said at the end of prayers
which contain a petition; we must remember,
however, that these prayers conclude with a
doxology, and it is to this that the Amen is a response.
The Amen with which some preachers conclude their
sermons was likewise originally the Amen
terminating a doxology and was perhaps said by the
hearers. (We saw above that "to preach" originally
meant not only to explain or demonstrate, but also to

proclaim God's praises.) The doxologies scattered throughout St. Paul's letters all end with "Amen" (e.g., Rom. 11:36; 15:33; 16:24, 27).

In the Apocalypse, "Amen" concludes the doxologies in the prologue (Apoc 1:6, 7); it even occurs at the beginning of a doxology, where, clearly, it cannot mean "So be it" (Apoc. 7:11). In the heavenly liturgy the four living creatures answer "Amen" to all creation's praise of God and the Lamb (Apoc. 5:14). Furthermore, the Apocalypse associates *Amen* with *Alleluia* (Apoc. 19:4). (Later on, St. Augustine would tell a somewhat surprised audience that we will spend eternity repeating "Amen! Alleluia!," since these two words alone can give expression to our intuition of God's majesty and to the joy we will feel.)

The Apocalypse contains a further, quite extraordinary text concerning Amen. For Christ himself is called "the Amen, the faithful Witness and true, the Source of God's creation" (Apoc. 3:14). He is in his very person the loving, enthusiastic affirmation which concludes and sums up the thanksgiving that brings all creation to the Father. He is the eternal "yes" of those creatures who give themselves to the Father to whom they owe everything. St. Paul had already made the same point: "Jesus Christ, whom Silvanus, Timothy, and I preached to you as Son of God, was not alternately 'yes' and 'no'; he was never anything but 'yes.' Whatever promises God has made have been fulfilled in him; therefore it is through him that we address our Amen to God when we worship together" (2 Cor. 1:19-20).

In addition to the Amen which forms a solemn conclusion for the Eucharistic Prayer, there is another very important one which the faithful are to speak out clearly: their "Amen" at Communion, with its very rich meaning. The priest extends the consecrated bread to the communicant with the words "The body of Christ," and the believer, before receiving it, answers "Amen."

This Amen is first of all an act of faith in the real presence of Christ: "Yes, I firmly believe that the body of Christ is present under the outward form of this consecrated bread." But "the body of Christ" is also the Church, which has been brought into existence through baptism and is nourished and unified by the Eucharist (cf. Col. 1:18). The communicant's "Amen," therefore, expresses not only a profession of faith but a commitment of love: "Yes, I want to be one with the Body of Christ and to work at building it up through my Christian life, and especially through brotherly love." St. Augustine preached many sermons on the theme: "Become the 'Amen' which you say."[4] The act of communicating, therefore, does not consist simply in "receiving the host." For, here again, the faithful are invited to share actively in the Eucharistic celebration and to exercise their baptismal priesthood.

---

[1]The Greek verb and its Latin equivalent, *gratias agere,* suggest a link that is lost in English for the Greek *charis* and Latin *gratia* mean "grace of God" as well as "thanks." (The same connection is more remotely echoed in English in the phrase "to say grace [i.e., thanks] before or after meals.") The act of rendering thanks to God can, in fact, be done only under the influence of grace; God gives his grace and we acknowledge it and echo it back in giving thanks.

[2]In Matthew 26:26 and Mark 14:22 it is said that Jesus "spoke the blessing" as he took the bread at the Last Supper.

[3]The word is derived from the Greek words *doxa* (glory) and *logos* (word, discourse); a "doxology" is an acclamation to the glory of God.

[4]Cf. M. Huftier, "Corpus Christi. Amen," *La vie spirituelle,* 111 (July-December, 1964), pp. 477-502.

4.

The Offering

Our thanksgiving must not remain purely interior. It is expressed first of all in the offering of bread and wine to God.

WHAT DOES "OFFERING" MEAN?

What exactly does the verb "to offer" mean? It means "to put out, to carry forward." Such is the original meaning of the verb "to offer" (Latin: *ob* = in front of, and *ferre* = to carry, bear), and of the nouns "oblation," "offering." The corresponding Greek term, used by the Eastern Christians to designate the essential part of the Mass, is *anaphora*, which means "a carrying up" or "a raising up." Both words — the Greek and the Latin-English — involve, in addition, the idea of exchange.

The offering of bread and wine in the Eucharist has, therefore, a very precise and very material meaning. In human language God is always regarded as enthroned on high; his gifts descend from above. Therefore, if we want to show our gratitude and to attempt — impossible though the task is — to pay our debt by some kind of exchange, we will raise up or carry aloft our gifts. Recall how the priest, before praying the great prayer of thanksgiving, the Preface, invites the faithful: "Lift up your hearts!" God, of course, being pure spirit, is both everywhere and nowhere; but nothing can prevent men who live in a world of matter and imagination from representing him to themselves as one who dwells in the heights. In the *Gloria* we sing: "Glory to God in the highest," and in the *Sanctus:* "Hosanna in the highest."

It is easily seen, then, why the priest, at the beginning of the Eucharistic sacrifice proper, elevates the plate holding the bread to be consecrated, as well as the cup containing the wine.

It would be a serious mistake, however, to think that once this gesture has been made, the act of offering is ended. In fact, the Mass in its entirety is an offering, that is, a raising up of our gifts. When the bishop ordains a new priest and lists his main functions, he says quite simply, with reference to the Mass: ". . . it is the priest's duty to offer . . . ," and in the context this simple word means to celebrate Mass. So too, after the consecration of the Mass, the priest recites the prayer of anamnesis, or remembrance, in which the main thought is "we offer." It is not enough, then, simply to make the body and blood of the sacrificed Jesus present on the altar through the consecration; they must also be offered to the Father.

THE ELEVATIONS

There are four "elevations" during the course of the Mass. The first one occurs in presenting the gifts to God; it is a quite restrained gesture. The second follows the consecration of the bread and then of the wine; now that the altar faces the people, this double elevation enables the people to respond spontaneously with their own personal acts of faith and devotion to the essential act of offering in the consecration that has just taken place before their eyes. The third elevation concludes the Eucharistic Prayer and is accompanied by the words: "Through him, with him, in him. . . ." This gesture is a most solemn act of offering to God, summing up the whole sacrifice, and it is, consequently, a climactic point in the action. Finally, before receiving Communion himself and then giving it to others, the priest once again raises the consecrated bread in order to show it to the people. This elevation is done in the Eastern rites also. We must add that before giving the Host to each individual communicant, the priest raises it slightly to show it to him and says: "The body of Christ."

THE WHOLE MASS IS AN OFFERING

What we now call "the preparation of the gifts" used to be called "the Offertory." The word is now kept only for the optional song which accompanies the preparation and should no longer be used to describe this opening part of the Eucharistic liturgy, for it is equivocal. This initial act is not the moment of authentic offering. Undoubtedly we do offer and present the bread and wine, to God for they are ours and we bring them for the sacrifice. But this first offering is only a beginning, an indispensable condition. The bread and wine are not going to remain such; God is going to take them and make of them the body and blood of his Son. Then Jesus, on the occasion of, and under the appearances of, this now consecrated bread and wine, will offer himself to the Father. There we have the truly essential act of offering. We say, after all, do we not, that the Mass is the offering and immolation of Jesus Christ to his Father for the salvation of the world? Jesus offered and immolated himself at the Last Supper and on the Cross. That is the offering which the Mass renews. The essential act of offering, therefore, takes place at the consecration.

WE MUST OFFER OURSELVES AT MASS

The Mass does not end with the consecration, however. It continues with prayers and actions that too often go unexplained. It is not enough for Christ to offer himself invisibly. In the visible sphere it is the Church, in the person of the priest and the faithful, that offers the sacrifice.

Now the purpose of the prayers which follow upon the consecration is to permit the Church to offer Christ's sacrifice and to offer herself with him. Christ, after all, is never alone. Since Calvary and Pentecost, he has made all men, and especially the baptized (that is, the Catholic Church), the Body of which he is the Head. The head cannot but take its body with it wherever it goes. At Mass, therefore, it is not Christ alone who offers and is offered; the Church too (that is, all of us) offers, offers herself, and is offered with Christ: "Look with favor on your Church's offering, and see the Victim whose death has reconciled us to yourself."[1]

These reflections can surely help to correct any improper way of thinking or acting in regard to the Eucharist and the Mass. The Mass cannot be regarded as a sacrifice offered by Christ exclusively, with ourselves being called upon simply to look on and to pray that we may benefit from its fruits. If that were the truth of the matter, then it would make little difference whether or not our thoughts were occupied with other matters while we were at Mass. Furthermore, if the Mass were only Christ's sacrifice, why should there be any need to be present at it? Wouldn't it be enough for a few priests to celebrate it in various places? Whether we were present or stayed at home, the sacrifice of Christ would not be celebrated any more or any less. If, however, the Mass involves the whole Church offering Christ and offering herself with him, we can readily understand why all the baptized should assist at Mass — not simply being there as passive spectators, but associating themselves with it and actively sharing in it.

Do we not also tend to think of the Eucharist too exclusively in terms of Communion, that is, of the descent of a splendid divine gift to us which we need only receive? Yet if the Eucharist is primarily a thanksgiving and an offering, it is not simply a descent of God to man, but also an ascent of man to God. It is not enough simply to receive. We must also give ourselves; we must offer ourselves.

Self-offering is indeed the basic act of the religious soul. God wants us to offer ourselves, to give ourselves to him. He is not content to have our respect, our obedience, even our prayers, if in respecting and obeying and praying we continue to be our own masters, shut up, as it were, within ourselves. The Mass does not require us simply to offer bread and wine as material, lifeless objects. It does not require us simply to offer Christ, who is undoubtedly adorable but also distinct from us. It invites us to give ourselves, for the simple reason that it is the sacrament of charity, of love. There is no love, however, if a person is satisfied with giving an external possession, however valuable. It has been said that alms-giving is a subtle form of contempt; the accusation is valid if a person is content to give money without giving any of his heart. Love does not consist in giving; it consists in giving oneself. In dying on the Cross, Jesus was not giving anything external to himself, but he gave his whole self. Had he not instructed us: "There is no greater love than this: to lay down one's life for one's friends" (John 15:13)?

This gift or offering of ourselves is the ultimate purpose of the Mass, the mysterious realm into which it leads us. We are told as much by Vatican II's document on the liturgy:

> The Church . . . earnestly desires that Christ's faithful. . . . should participate, knowingly, devoutly, and actively. . . . By offering the Immaculate Victim, not only through the hands of the priest, but also with him, they should learn to offer themselves too. Through Christ the Mediator, they should be drawn day by day into ever closer union with God and with each other, so that finally God may be all in all.[2]

[1] Third Eucharistic Prayer.

[2] Vatican II, *Constitution on the Sacred Liturgy*, no. 48, in Walter M. Abbott (ed.), *The Documents of Vatican II* (New York: Herder and Herder, Association Press, 1966), p. 154.

5.

The Exchange

The Eucharist is the sacrament of giving. It is this in a double direction: it is the sacrament of God's gift to men, and the sacrament of men's gift to God.

GOD'S GIFT TO MEN

God gives himself to men. This short sentence contains the whole difference between an abstract idea of God and the revelation which God has given us of himself in Scripture. A philosopher may, by reflection, reach the conception of a supreme Being, a Creator and Master of the universe, and even a Providence. The Jews, however, who had the personal revelation of the one God, knew that this God was filled with concern for them, even with tender love. For the God of the Old Testament, despite the often repeated statement, was not primarily a God who inspired fear; many passages of the Pentateuch, the prophets, and the Psalms show him to be a fatherly and very kind God (cf., e.g., Exod. 34:6; Is. 54:4-10; Ezek. 34:11-16; Hos. 2:16-22; Pss. 103: 145:8-9).

It was reserved to Jesus Christ, however, to bring us the gospel, that is, the joyful, incredible news of God's "gift" to men. This "gift" is his very self. As St.

John puts it in one of the most staggering sentences in the Gospel: "God so loved the world that he gave his only Son" (John 3:16). That is the basis, as it were, for the mystery of the Incarnation, of God becoming man. On God's part, there is such an outflow, such an over-flow of goodness toward mankind that he gives himself to it, uniting himself to it in the most intimate way possible — he espouses human nature in such a way as to be one with it, in the unity of a single person, our Lord Jesus Christ, truly man and truly God.

Jesus Christ is in the fullest sense a gift of God to men. Being God, he has been given to us gratuitously, without any right or merit on our part. Moreover, he has not been simply shown to us or loaned to us; he has been given to us, he belongs to us, he is ours, possessing our human nature, our flesh with all its weaknesses except sin, and having experience of poverty, weariness, hunger and thirst, betrayal and death. He shared the meals of men and, like men, was finally laid in a grave.

Once he had returned to heaven, Jesus did not leave us orphans, but gave us his Spirit, the Holy Spirit, one of whose names is "Gift." The Holy Spirit causes God to dwell in us, for the Holy Spirit is love. This permanent presence and life of God abiding in us through the Spirit is called "grace." Grace is what Jesus was speaking of when he said to the Samaritan woman: "If only you recognized God's gift!" To this woman, who so longed for love but found it only in sin, which is the caricature and poison of love, Jesus offers the love which quenches thirst instead of increasing it: "If only you recognized God's gift, and who it is that is asking you for a drink, you would have asked him instead, and he would have given you living water. . . . Whoever drinks the water I give him will never be thirsty; no, the water I give shall become a fountain within him, leaping to provide eternal life" (John 4:10-15).

We come now to the Eucharist. It sums up and contains all God's gifts to men. In it Jesus Christ is really present and is given to us so completely that he becomes our very food. In the same words in which he affirms his presence, Jesus also says that he gives himself: "Take this, all of you, and eat it: this is my body which will be given up for you." The Eucharist gives us Jesus Christ immolated, that is to say, completely given: "There is no greater love than this: to lay down one's life for one's friends." It does not give us simply his immolation, but Jesus himself in his entirety, with his body and soul, his blood, his humanity and divinity, and all his mysteries.

Finally, in Communion Jesus is given to us not simply that we may eat his flesh (for, as he says in this context, "the flesh is useless" — John 6:63), but that we may be filled with the spirit and grace. In the splendid Second Vespers Magnificat antiphon for the Office of Corpus Christi, St. Thomas Aquinas has us sing: "O holy Banquet, in which Christ is received, the memory of his Passion is renewed, the soul is filled with grace, and a pledge of future glory is given." Here we see how the Eucharist is, more than any other reality, the gift of God to men. For, while all the sacraments are gifts of God, this one surpasses them all and sums them all up, really containing, as it does, the Gift of gifts — Jesus Christ.

MEN'S GIFT TO GOD

If the Eucharist is God's gift to men, it is also men's gift to God. Did you notice that in Jesus' conversation with the Samaritan woman, before saying to her: "If only you recognized God's gift," Jesus first asks her: "Give me a drink"?

God gives to us; he gives himself to us. But he also wants us to give to him, to give ourselves to him. His gift is not an invisible one; it is his Son made man, visible in our midst. In like fashion, we cannot be satisfied to give him a purely spiritual gift. The gift must be visible, a sign, that is, a sacrament. This sacramental sign is the Eucharist. We give God our presence at Mass, our songs, our prayers, bread and wine. It is true, of course, as we have already observed, that all these things were first given to us by God. Thus the Fourth Eucharistic Prayer can say: "Lord, look upon this sacrifice which you have given to your Church."

THE COLLECTION

In olden days at Rome, the gift of the faithful to God was given in an especially meaningful way. The people came in procession to the altar, carrying not only bread and wine, but oil, wax, and the new fruits of the harvest. A portion of these gifts was consecrated and thus directly involved in the sacrifice. A second portion was used to aid the poor, a third was for the sustenance of the clergy. The liturgy has preserved the memory of these various gifts. Thus in the Mass texts, the bread and wine, even after the consecration, are often called "gifts" and "presents," because we do not forget that they have been supplied by the faithful.

We can, of course, still practice this procession of offerings in which the faithful used to bring their gifts to the altar. But we should not forget that the ceremony has been retained in a simplified and obviously more prosaic form — the collection. There is every justification, of course, for protesting against endlessly multiplied and injudicious collections, but it would be wrong to want to eliminate the collection entirely from the Mass. It is, in fact, an integral part of the celebration, and we should see in it, not a sordid necessity, but a religious gesture and, once again, a sign. The important thing is not the amount we give but our inner generosity. When Jesus saw a poor widow putting a very small coin into the Temple treasury, he said: "I assure you, this poor widow has put in more than all the rest. They make contributions out of their surplus, but she from her want has given what she could not afford — every penny she had to live on" (Luke 21:1-4).

In the "Offertory" section of his poem "La Messa là-bas," Paul Claudel puts these words on the celebrant's lips: "They are holding out the plate to you — have you naught but this wretched sou, this nameless dirty coin? Is yours the only purse that opens? . . . Why do you rob our God of what is his very own?"[1]

THE EXCHANGES IN THE INCARNATION AND THE MASS

If we offer God bread and wine, and then the body and blood of Christ which are present in these signs, we expect God in return to pour out all kinds of blessings on us. In this way the Mass is an exchange. The liturgy often uses this last term in the Prayers over the Gifts, in which we ask for benefits in return for what we offer. For example: "Lord God, by this holy exchange of gifts you share with us your divine life. Grant that everything we do may be directed by the knowledge of your truth."[2] Or again: "Lord, accept this sacrifice, and through this holy exchange of gifts free us from the sins that enslave us."[3]

In the ancient Roman liturgy, the exchanges practiced in the Mass were very obvious, and, without turning into archeologists, we can still find evidence of them today. The faithful came to the altar in procession twice. On the first occasion, at the Offertory, they came to present their gifts. After the sacrifice, they came again, in the same order, to take back their gifts, but these had now been changed. The faithful who had offered simple bread and wine now received in exchange the body and blood of Christ. They had brought such offerings as men can bring; they received back the bread of eternal life and the cup of salvation. It was a genuine exchange, but how very much in their favor! No one ever loses by exchanging with God; to the generous giver he gives back a hundredfold and more!

The idea of exchange is already present in the basic mystery of Christianity, the Incarnation. God and man are no longer separated by an impassable abyss. Between the two a bridge has been built, a commerce — in the noblest sense of the word — has been established. The Church sings of this in one of the most beautiful antiphons of the Christmas season: *O admirabile commercium!* O marvelous exchange! The Creator of our race has deigned to take a body and soul to himself and be born of the Virgin; and thus becoming man without a human father, has bestowed on us his own divinity."[4] The same idea recurs in a Christmas prayer: "Grant that we may become sharers in his divinity who took to himself our humanity."[5] The Mass only continues and perfects this exchange. For here our bread and wine, our human gifts, become the flesh and blood of the God-Man and are then returned to us to become our own flesh and blood, and so to divinize us.

THE PLACE OF EXCHANGES IN HUMAN LIFE

These considerations may seem somewhat forced. Yet we must observe that without exchange there can be no life, not even on the physiological level. Without exchange there is no social life, no cultural and intellectual life.

What, after all, is the nutrition and growth of a plant but an exchange with the earth in which it is rooted and which it will someday enrich in turn by its decomposition? What is breathing but an exchange? A being wholly closed in upon itself, borrowing nothing from the milieu in which it lives and restoring nothing to it, could neither grow nor develop. The stones engage in no exchanges, but every living thing lives by exchange.

What is teaching, intellectual culture, literary or artistic life, reading, and conversation but an exchange of ideas? What is trade or social life but an exchange of services? A society is not healthy when injustice rules and it is always the same people who give and the same people (a different group!) who receive, without any genuine exchange taking place between capital and labor, artisans and intellectuals, the simple and the learned. A family is alive and happy only if the law of exchange is at work in it. Of course, children receive everything from their parents, but they have a duty to repay what they can, initially in the form of affection and respect, later in the form of support and help.

In the same way, there is no spiritual life without exchange. A soul closed in upon itself and looking for nothing from a higher being is a dead soul. A soul which prays to God only in order to receive benefits from him, but which never thanks and praises him, is a soul with a very weak and mediocre life. Here we can see the unqualified necessity for prayer. Prayer is not a self-interested, humiliating act of begging. True prayer is a continual exchange with God. It has aptly been defined as the soul's breathing. As the body breathes through an exchange in the twofold movement of aspiration and expiration, so the soul too breathes when it draws God in by its petitions and then gives something of his blessings back to him in the form of thanksgiving and praise.

Our Lord taught us the power of prayer by means of a parable that must be read in its entirety if it is to be properly understood.[6] Christ offers as a model the man who knocks on his friend's door in the middle of the night looking for bread. The man in bed finally gets up so that he may have some peace and quiet. Jesus next suggests the picture of a child who asks his father for food and who will certainly not be given a stone instead of bread, or a scorpion instead of an egg, or a snake instead of a fish. Now if we read no further than this, we might think that one who prays should ask of God only temporal blessings or self-centered benefits. We should read to the end: "If you, with all your sins, know how to give your children good things, how much more will the heavenly Father give the Holy Spirit to those who ask him." That's right, the Holy Spirit! Authentic prayer does not mean asking God for this or that — happiness, success, health, or even eternal salvation; it means asking for the Holy Spirit. "Spirit" is breath and inspiration. As one of the psalms says: "I gasp with open mouth in my yearning for your commands" (Ps. 119:131). Prayer gives us this mysterious breath, the good and holy Spirit who will enable us to breathe with God and to live in a state of exchange with him.

THE MASS, SCHOOL OF PERFECT PRAYER

We can now see how the Mass is a school of perfect prayer. For the Mass is not a uniform movement but a perpetual give-and-take. At the beginning we celebrate God's praises in the Entrance Song. After the greeting we ask pardon for our sins in the penitential rite. Next we glorify God in the *Gloria* and ask for his help in the Opening Prayer. We receive the teaching of his word in the Readings, and meditate on it, savoring its sweetness, in the Responsorial Psalm. We listen to the Gospel and express our acceptance of it in the Creed; we make petition for the needs of the whole world in the Prayer of the Faithful, and bring our gifts to the altar. All that follows is a closely woven web of thanksgiving and petitions for all the needs of the Church. Once Christ has been given to us in the consecration, we offer him to the Father for the latter's glory. Finally, we receive Christ as our food, and the Mass ends with a last thanksgiving. Thus the Mass is a ceaseless exchange, a constant give-and-take, a ladder more sublime and mysterious than that of Jacob, which "rested on the ground, with its top reaching to the heavens; and God's messengers were going up and down on it. And there was the Lord standing beside him" (Gen. 28:12).

For the moment I have left aside that exchange, likewise indispensable, which must take place between brothers in Christ through love. Let us note simply that the Mass teaches us to break through the crust of egoism that too often covers our sluggish souls, and to enter into a vital exchange with our God, who is not simply a Master to be adored and petitioned but also a Father who gives us life and expects our love in return.

[1]Paul Claudel, "La Messe là-bas," *Oeuvre poetique* (Paris: Gallimard, 1967), pp. 502–503.

[2]Prayer over the Gifts for the Fifth Sunday of Easter.

[3]Prayer over the Gifts for Wednesday in the Second Week of Lent.

[4]First Antiphon for Vespers for the Solemnity of Mary, the Holy Mother of God (Octave of the Nativity of the Lord).

[5]The priest used to say this prayer at every Mass (with the addition of the words "through the mystery of this water and wine") as he put a drop of water into the chalice of wine; the prayer is still said at this point, but in shortened form. But it was originally a Collect for the Mass of Christmas Day and has been restored in its original form in the new Liturgy of the Hours for Christmas.

[6]Luke 11:5-13 (Gospel for the Seventeenth Sunday in Ordinary Time, Series C).

6.

Brotherly Love

EUCHARISTIC BODY AND MYSTICAL BODY

We saw in the first chapter of this book that the Mass is, most obviously, the action of a community, the Church. Even today, unfortunately, the word "Church" makes us think of a material building or an administrative structure. Or people think of the Church as simply the clergy with its complex hierarchy, its various religious Orders, etc. In fact, the true idea of the Church is much simpler, much more comprehensive, and much more beautiful. The first chapter of Vatican II's *Dogmatic Constitution on the Church* reminds us of this in a magnificent way. The Church is the assembly of all the baptized, who are so closely united as to form not only a single society or family but a single spiritual organism, and even, in St. Paul's striking phrase, a single body. The head of this body is Christ; its soul, the Holy Spirit.

Two sacraments form the body. The first is baptism, which admits us into this body, one after another as the generations unroll. For each individual the incorporation takes place once and for all in baptism — or rather it is begun in baptism. A second sacrament, the Eucharist, renews the unity daily and makes it ever more intimate. The Eucharist is the sacrament of unity and the sacrifice of the Church, that is, of the assembly of Christians. The Prayer over the Gifts for the feast of Corpus Christi states the point briefly and clearly: "Lord, may the bread and cup we offer bring your Church the unity and peace they signify." The consecrated gifts indeed represent and contain the physical body of Christ, but, more mysteriously still, they re-present and contain what we call his Mystical Body, that is, the unity of Christians in Christ.

THE EUCHARIST, SACRAMENT OF BROTHERLY LOVE

We must note, moreover, that when the expression "Mystical Body" was first used, it meant precisely the Eucharistic body of Christ. The phrase eventually came to refer to the union of Christians, because this union is the effect ultimately re-presented and produced by the Eucharist.[1]

The relation between the Mass and the Church is thus an essential one. For the Mass gathers the Church together; the Mass makes the Church, just as the Church offers the Mass and offers itself in the Mass.

All this amounts to saying that the Mass is the sacrament, and effects the mystery, of brotherly love. The Church is not an ordinary society whose unity is the result of external laws. It is a society grounded in love. Its head and source of unity, Christ, does not derive his power solely from an authority to command, but from his own pre-eminence in love as well. Christ gathers men together because he loved them to the utmost and gave them the greatest proof of love — he died for them. The great commandment which he left his followers, precisely at the moment when he instituted the Eucharist and celebrated the first Mass, was to love one another as he had loved them.

THE RITES OF THE MASS WHICH SIGNIFY LOVE AND BRING IT INTO PLAY

This basic truth about the Mass throws light on numerous elements of its celebration. To begin with, the Mass is not the action of an isolated individual; it is a coming together. When the faithful are asked to form a group around the altar, to sing together, to answer the priest in unison, to adopt the same postures, the reason is not just to give greater vitality and beauty to the services; it is primarily because the sacrament of unity should take form in a union of bodies, voices, and postures which will both express and foster a union of hearts.

Why was it, in the early Church, that at the moment when the Eucharist proper was to begin, the catechumens, Jews, pagans, and public sinners were dismissed from the service? It was because the sacrament of unity could be celebrated only by those whom baptism had introduced into the community and who had not separated themselves from the community by serious sin.

Why did the congregation solemnly recite the Our Father as Communion time approached? Because this prayer does not say "My Father" but "Our Father," thereby implying that we are all brothers. It was recited, furthermore, because in it we say: "Forgive us our trespasses as we forgive those who trespass against us." We may not receive the Eucharistic Communion if our hearts are resentful, jealous, or contemptuous of others. According to some first-rank theologians, what makes a Communion sacrilegious is not the fact of receiving the holy Christ into a soul that is stained with sin; the glorious Christ, after all, cannot be contaminated, so how could an unclean soul in any way soil the impassible, resurrected body of Christ? What makes the Communion sacrilegious is the terrible lie of approaching the sacrament of unity while continuing to be attached to one's sins, for sin is a division, a lack of loving union with God and our brothers.

The whole preparation for Communion, beginning with the Lord's Prayer, is intended to remind us of the central duty of brotherly love. Thus the ceremony of the breaking of the bread is deeply meaningful in regard to unity. In the allegorical interpretations of past centuries, the fraction was seen as a symbol of the Passion. Yet St. John carefully remarks that in the case of Jesus, as in the case of the passover lamb, the prescription was observed: "Break none of his bones" (John 19:36; cf. Exod. 12:46 and Num. 9:12)! The rite we are discussing here has never been called "the breaking of Christ," but only "the breaking of bread." The action must therefore be interpreted by reference to the simple yet immensely meaningful gesture of the father at table sharing one loaf among all his children.

Some of the fragments of the broken bread used to serve as *fermentum*, or "leaven" (of unity and love). Acolytes like St. Tarcisius used to carry the fragments, in linen bags suspended from the neck, to other priests and bishops, often close by but sometimes at a distance, who would join the bread thus received to the bread of their own sacrifice. In this way two bishops would show that they were "in communion," an expression which thus has a very concrete meaning.

Before Communion the kiss of peace was given at the altar and then exchanged by all the faithful with one another. It represented an application of the Lord's bidding, and had even been practiced, in an earlier day, at the Offertory in order to give stricter obedience to the words of the Gospel: "If you bring your gift to the altar and there recall that your brother has anything against you, leave your gift at the altar, go first to be reconciled with your brother, and then come and offer your gift" (Matthew 5:23-24). The new Order of Mass makes allowance for the introduction of some sort of peace gesture upon the recommendation of the bishops of a given country. The bishops of the United States have not as yet approved any such procedure for the kiss of peace.

Everyone used to come to the altar — the only one in the church in those days — in procession (a sign of unity) and while singing (another sign of unity and love). To organize a solemn, and orderly procession of communicants would require nothing more than a simple exercise of the "ministry of orderliness." Such a procession would bring home to the faithful that Eucharistic Communion is a rite which both expresses and gives new reality to brotherly love and ecclesial unity.

DOES PAUL'S CENSURE OF THE CORINTHIANS TOUCH US?

For centuries down until the new lectionary was introduced a few years ago, the New Testament reading at Mass on Holy Thursday and Corpus Christi was the passage in which St. Paul recalls the details of Christ's institution of the Eucharist at the Last

Supper. St. Paul did not write this doctrinal passage simply to elaborate a theoretical teaching; he did so in order to react against the abuses which prevailed in the Church at Corinth. At that time a rite called the "agape" was still being practiced there; it has now disappeared. The Greek word *agapē* means "brotherly love" or "charity". It also used to signify a fraternal meal which the faithful took together and which ended with the celebration of the Eucharist. By this time the fraternal meal had lost its proper character. People were eating at little tables instead of sharing everything in brotherly fashion, rich and poor alike. Some were stuffing themselves, while others were going hungry. In these circumstances, says St. Paul, it cannot be said that you are celebrating the Lord's Supper, for you are seriously lacking in charity (1 Cor. 11:17-22).

We calmly read this passage today as a revelation of a historical oddity. The agape is now only a memory. The Eucharist is celebrated in a church and has no connection with ordinary meals. On the contrary, since the obligation of communicating while fasting has been imposed to prevent the recurrence of the kind of abuse Paul describes, is it not part of our problem that we see in the Mass a self-enclosed ceremony? Does not this explain the little influence Catholics have in the world? We live like everyone else. We come to a church to be present, perhaps very devoutly, at a majestic and mysterious ceremony. When it is over, we return home to lead the same life as before, just like our neighbor's, and perhaps even less virtuous. We have celebrated the mystery of unity and received the sacrament of brotherly love within the four walls of the church according to carefully regulated, preordained rites. But the whole thing has no repercussions in our real life. We have sung in chorus and approached the holy table with people whose names we perhaps do not know and whose difficulties we do not even seek to discover. We let these other people, whom in theory we have treated as brothers, go home in their poverty, perhaps even in destitution, while we ourselves go home to a good meal.

Paul's accusation against the baptized at Corinth nineteen hundred years ago, far from being out of date, is cruelly relevant: "When you assemble it is not to eat the Lord's Supper, for everyone is in haste to eat his own supper. One person goes hungry while another gets drunk" (1 Cor. 11:20-21).

Through our fault, then, there is a risk of the Mass being emptied of its power if we turn it merely into a form of spiritual consolation for selfish, well-fed parishioners. The Eucharist bears its proper fruit and has its proper meaning only if it stirs us to limitless pity for the world's distress, to an insatiable hunger for justice and love. If our churches are so sparsely filled in comparison with the vast numbers who remain outside, is it not because we have turned what ought to be the leaven of love into a conventional, dead ceremony? In the face of contemporary unbelief, can we hear without trembling Christ's words to his Father, praying "that they may be one, as we are one. . . . So shall the world know that you sent me" (John 17:22-23)?

---

[1]Cf. Henri de Lubac, "Corpus Mysticum: L'Eucharistie et l'Église au moyen-âge," *Theologie,* 3 (Paris: Aubier, 2nd ed., 1949).

7.

Love of God

Brotherly love, or fraternal charity, is only the second commandment; it is like the first, says our Lord, and derives from it. The first commandment is: "You shall love the Lord your God with all your heart, with all your soul, with all your mind, and with all your strength." And this is the second, Jesus adds: "You shall love your neighbor as yourself" (Mark 12:30-31). Without love of our brothers, love of God risks being either hypocritical or unreal. But without love of God, love of neighbor risks being simply natural goodness, philanthropy, or even a somewhat contemptuous pity.

This is a Gospel teaching which people today have great difficulty in accepting. "If you love me because of God," they will say, "you do not love me for myself. But I don't want to be loved in such a chance way!" The objection stems from an inadequate idea of God. Of course, that is the source of all objections against God, notably those aimed at the compatibility of human freedom with divine omnipotence. People think of God as though he were a creature — a greater and more powerful one indeed, but, in the last analysis,

56

belonging to the same category as we do. In that case, the love you have for God is in the same category as the love you have for your brother; then when you love your brother because of God, you do not seem to be loving your brother for his own sake.

We must realize, therefore, that God is infinitely superior to all creatures and cannot be put in a series with them. He is not alongside them nor even, in the strict sense of the word, above them; rather, he enfolds or contains them. All that I am I owe to God. All that I am is in God. No one can reach me except through God. No one can truly love me without loving God, because all that is good in me, all that is deserving of love in me, belongs to God. To use a very accurate formula of the spiritual writers, it is less a matter of loving one's brother because of God or second to God than of loving him *in God*.

The first commandment is to love God, and we must admit that it is extremely difficult to fulfill. The reason is quite simple: we are not angels, those pure spirits who live in an invisible world and are nourished by an invisible food. We have a body, and the body is not a burden or a disguise, but our *very self*. Even our most sublime ideas come to us only from what we see and touch. If that is true of knowledge, how much truer is it of love! What draws our love is the immediate, the visible, the sensuous. If so few men love God, the reason is that God is invisible.

The point has been very well put in the splendid Collect for the Twentieth Sunday in Ordinary Time: "O God, you have stored up invisible blessings for those who love you" [the invisibility of which makes it so difficult to love you]. Fill our hearts now with fervent love for you [love for God is such a sublime thing that it cannot arise in us spontaneously but must be instilled in us by God], so that loving you in all else and beyond all else, we may win your promised rewards, which surpass our deepest desires." This translation attempts to give accurately the content of the official Latin text of the Roman Catholic Church: "Deus, qui diligentibus te bona invisibilia praeparasti, infunde cordibus nostris tui amoris affectum, ut, te in omnibus et super omnia diligentes, promissiones tuas, quae omne desiderium superant, consequamur. Per Dominum." It is immediately evident that the version found in the American Sacramentary is a transmogrification of this profoundly theological and beautiful Roman Collect.

LOVE OF THE INVISIBLE

In saying that we can love only what we see, I was rather hard on human nature. I did not mean that our love is directed only to immediate, sensible realities. Many men, after all, love, often passionately, invisible realities, such as their country, art, astronomy, or mathematics. But if we look closely, we will see that the immaterial object of love is embodied in material objects and that the love itself takes shape in actions and behavior. The man who loves his country sees it in its scenery, its land, its monuments, its people; his love is not passive contemplation but is exercised in, and grows through, the services he renders his country, sometimes in heroic fashion. The person who loves mathematics does not love an abstract goddess, a kind of allegorical figure representing science, or a white statue with empty eyes; rather, his mind finds delight as it moves among numbers, and he devotes a large part of his time to his studies. Well, the same thing holds, in due proportion, for love of God.

God has commanded us to love him. But he has also furnished all kinds of visible objects for our love and all kinds of practices by which we can prove and develop our love for him. Among the Jews, who themselves had already received the command to love God, this love was directed with great fervor to the Law, the Temple, Jerusalem, and the Chosen People.

GOD BECOME VISIBLE, EASIER TO LOVE

In Christianity the love of God has become infinitely easier, for God himself became man in order to render himself visible and closer to us. The first Preface for Christmas sings of this: "In the wonder of the incarnation your eternal Word has brought to the eyes of faith a new and radiant vision of your glory. In him we see our God made visible and so are caught up in love of the God we cannot see."

This incarnate God, Jesus Christ, was not satisfied simply to show himself to us and thus enable us to see God in him. He acted and spent himself for our salvation. He gave us the greatest proof of love, which is to sacrifice one's life for those one loves. Knowing, then, beyond all doubt that God loves us in infinite measure, how can we fail to love him in return with all that is in us?

You may object: But all that took place in the distant past! The crucifix, which so clearly shows us Christ's love for men, pictures an event of long ago. Christ has returned to heaven. He did become incarnate, but now he is invisible again!

Here is where we discover the Eucharist anew and understand how it is the sacrament of God's love. Jesus indeed did return to heaven, yet he remains among us. God continues to be visible, but under the veil of the sacramental mystery. That which is only a memory in the crucifix, is a living reality in the Eucharist. For the Christ who is present under the outward appearances of consecrated bread is not solely nor chiefly the Jesus of the manger; it is Jesus crucified and risen for us so that we might pass from death to life. As St. Paul says: "Every time, then, you eat this bread and drink this cup, you proclaim the death of the Lord until he comes!" (1 Cor. 11:26). Christ instituted this sacrament on the eve of his Passion in order that it might be both the memorial and the summing up of all his love for us. St. John opens his account of the Last Supper with these words: "Before the feast of Passover, Jesus realized that the hour had come for him to pass from this world to the Father. He had loved his own in this world, and would show his love for them to the end" (John 13:1).

THE EUCHARIST COMMUNICATES THE
LOVE OF GOD TO US

It is not enough to say that the Eucharist is the sacrament of love of God because it recalls to us all that God has done for us. If the Eucharist were only that, we might perhaps be as well off fervently meditating before a piece of ordinary bread. But the Eucharist contains the living Christ and gives him to us as our food. Consequently, it does not simply show forth God's love to us; it also injects, as it were, those who receive it with love for God. This is why we are not simply to gaze upon, revere, and adore the Eucharist — we are to eat it. God is in it, and we come as near as we can to him, we absorb him, we are united to him, we are assimilated to him. Such gestures, such actions call for love and nourish it. For love acknowledges no distance; it seeks most intimate union and deepest assimilation. The first effect of the Eucharist is to intensify the love of God in us. Thus we ask in the Collect for the Thirtieth Sunday in Ordinary Time: "Almighty and eternal God, intensify our faith, hope and love. Teach us to love your commandments that we may reach your promised rewards — Omnipotens sempiterne Deus, da nobis fidei, spei et caritatis augmentum, et, ut mereamur assequi quo promittis, fac now amare quod praecipis."

Of course, all this takes place at very deep levels of our being. First communicants have often been deceived by being told that at the moment of receiving the Host they would feel their hearts inflamed by love for God; they have been disappointed and ashamed when nothing like that occurred. Love for God resides in depths which only rarely stir our sensible emotions. This is why love of God must always be accompanied by love of our brothers. If after communion our heart seems unmoved, that is of little consequence. But if we are willing to suffer and make sacrifices for the welfare of our brothers, then we do have the right to say that the love of God is in us: "No one has ever seen God. Yet if we love one another God dwells in us, and his love is brought to perfection in us" (1 John 4:12).

8.

Daily Bread

Love for God in a human heart is a fragile thing. The hardships, sorrows, and ugliness of life, our continually recurring egoism, the temptations that spring from so many sources — money, the flesh, ambition — all these weaken our love for God and the joy it brings, and cause us to slip back into sadness and boredom. We drag ourselves along life's way. It is for this very reason that the Eucharist is not, like baptism, a once-for-all sacrament — it is a daily meal. That is one of the reasons why this sacrament uses bread.

THE MANNA, ELIAS' BREAD,
AND THE MULTIPLICATION OF LOAVES

Sacred Scripture contains three prefigurations of the Eucharist in which we can see the aspect of daily strengthening that is the specific effect of bread in our daily life.

The Hebrew people had just been delivered from the inhuman life of slavery and forced labor to which they had been subjected in Egypt. Freed by the blood of the lamb and led by Moses, they cross the Red Sea. They had just emerged from the land of slavery. But they do not immediately enter the promised land of milk and honey. First they must wander about in the desert for forty years. Desert journeying is exhausting and discouraging. Men of the desert are nomads; they have no roof, no store of provisions, no security for the morrow. The Hebrews therefore begin to complain. They even have regretful longings for Egypt! True, they had been humiliated and unhappy there, but at least they had plenty of food to eat. What are they to eat in the wilderness?

At this point Moses prays, and God answers with a miracle. A mysterious substance falls from the sky each morning. At first the people are surprised and ask: "What is this?" (in Hebrew, *mān hū*, from which comes the name "manna"). They gather the heavenly food, enough for the day for each family (Exod. 16; Wis. of Sol. 16:20-21, 27-29). It is forbidden, indeed impossible, to provide for more than the immediate day, to lay in stores, for worms appear in what is left over from each day's supply. Besides, such precautions are needless, since God will unfailingly cause the manna to fall each morning. It will cease to fall only when the people have entered the promised land, which will supply all the food needed (Josh. 5:12). The manna was such a meaningful sign as a testimony to God's gifts and promises that the Hebrews kept a jarful of it in the Ark of the Covenant along with the tablets of the Law (Heb. 9:4).

Our Lord himself, in foretelling the coming gift of the Eucharist, spoke of the manna as a prefiguration of it (John 6:31, 49). It is easy to see how the manna is indeed such a figure. Deliverance through the blood of the lamb and the crossing of the Red Sea symbolize baptism, which delivers us from evil. But baptism does not, by itself, bring us into the promised land, into paradise. We still have ahead of us a long and toilsome

journey through the arid desert of earthly life. But
during that journey God nourishes us each morning,
if we wish it, with a heavenly food which daily restores
our strength and courage — the daily Bread which our
heavenly Father sends us. And when we finally enter
the promised land of heaven, the manna will no longer
fall; there will be no more Eucharist, for we will see
God face to face and he will nourish us continuously,
without intermediary or sacrament.

There is another figure of the Eucharist which St.
Thomas has highlighted in the Office for Corpus
Christi. The prophet Elias has been given a difficult
mission by God: he must resist King Ahab to his face
(1 Kings 19:1-8). Discouraged and exhausted, he runs
away, and while still in the desert, lies down on the
ground and prays to God: "This is enough, O Lord!
Take my life, for I am no better than my fathers."
Then he falls asleep under a broom tree. An angel
awakens him and says: "Get up and eat, else the
journey will be too long for you," while showing him a
hearth cake and a jug of water. Strengthened by this
food from heaven, Elias continues his journey and
walks for forty days until he reaches the mountain of
God, Mount Horeb. The bread given to Elias clearly
represents the Eucharist, which instills new courage
into us when we are cast down by the contradictions
and seeming absurdity of life. Being the sacrament of
love for God, it gives us the strength to climb that
steep mountain atop which we will find rest and peace
in God.

The third prefigurative event is part of Jesus' own
life. It is the episode of the multiplication of loaves. A
great crowd has followed Jesus into a wilderness area
where there is no way to supply them with food. But
Jesus says: "My heart is moved with pity for the

crowd. By now they have been with me three days, and have nothing to eat. I do not wish to send them away hungry, for fear they may collapse on the way" (Matthew 15:32). Then he works the miracle of multiplying the loaves. He will use this miracle as his point of departure for the great discourse in which he presents himself as the Bread of life and foretells the institution of the Eucharist (John 6:25-69).

From these three prefigurations we can see that the Eucharist is not a spiritual luxury, a delicacy intended for saints, but a substantial food which men need in order to overcome weakness and discouragement on the exhausting journey to the promised land and to God.

BREAD IN MAN'S LIFE

We can find still other reasons why the Eucharist was instituted with bread as its sacramental sign. Bread is man's regular daily food. It symbolizes his whole life and work. To earn one's bread means to earn one's living. This is all the more true inasmuch as bread is a food peculiar to man. Fruit and meat nourish us, of course, but they are also the food of animals, which only need to know how to graze, to gather, or to hunt. The making of bread, on the contrary, requires all kinds of activity of which only man is capable. To sow, harvest, thresh, grind, knead, and bake calls for experience and inventiveness, and for language by which to pass on these experiences and the discoveries. Bread therefore symbolizes man's life not only in its most elemental and instinctual aspects but also in its more properly intelligent and energetic dimensions. Consequently, when we offer bread to God, we are not simply offering his own gifts, but his gifts as transformed by our intelligent activity: "Blessed are you, Lord, God of all creation. Through your goodness we have this bread to offer, which earth has given and human hands have made."[1]

Bread also represents the human community. All the Fathers of the Church have noted that bread is composed of numerous grains which are reduced to unity by grinding, kneading, and baking. Moreover, we must point out that the making of a single piece of bread requires and symbolizes the collaboration of many different tradesmen: growers; bakers; millers; manufacturers of farm machines, mills, and ovens; suppliers of energy for machines, etc. Finally, when the bread reaches the table, the father of the family distributes it to his table-companions. All of them, by eating of the same loaf, literally communicate, i.e., share in what is common to all. Thus, apart from any consecration or supernatural intervention, bread already suggests union among men. It takes no great effort for us to understand that when the sacrament of bread becomes the sacrament of Christ's body, it is the sacrament of communion, of community, of the human family of which God is the Father, and Jesus the one who gathers them together.

JESUS, THE SEED PUT INTO THE GROUND

Finally, bread — wheat bread — has a still higher meaning. Jesus himself was compared to a grain of wheat. If the grain does not die, it remains by itself. But if it falls to the earth and dies, it produces much fruit (John 12:24). So, too, Jesus died for us and was put into the earth. Then, just as the grain returns to life, as it were, in the form of an ear in which the original single grain is seen to be multiplied, so Jesus, by dying and rising, has given birth to a multitude of brothers like himself, who in their turn must obey the same law of death, resurrection, and multiplication. All the varied activities required for the making of a piece of bread remind us of the labors Jesus had to undergo in order to give us the Eucharist. He had to humble himself in a human birth, die on the Cross, and after being put into the earth, rise again so that we might have the living and life-giving bread we call the Eucharist.[2]

We already see that the sacrament of bread is also the sacrament of sacrifice. This point will be more fully developed when we consider the Eucharist as the sacrament of the cup and the covenant. For the moment, let us simply note that the Eucharist is the sacrament not only of bread but of wine as well. This means that the Eucharist is a complete meal. Man needs not only food — he needs drink too. An advertising solgan reads: "A day without wine is a day without sunshine." Bread gives strength; wine gives delight (cf. Ps. 104:15). Christ wanted to refresh us wholly. In our earthly life, with its toil and sorrow, we need strength to fulfill our duties; but we also need joy if we are to fulfill them generously and cheerfully. The Eucharist, then, is not only the sacrament which enables us to work so as to win heaven; it is also the sacrament which fills our hearts so that we will be thankful to God.

---

[1]Prayer for the offering of the gifts at the beginning of the Liturgy of the Eucharist.
[2]"Living and life-giving bread *(panis vivus et vitalis)*" — hymn *Lauda Sion;* "Living bread, bestowing life on man *(panis vivus, vitam praestans homini)*" — hymn *Adoro te.*

9.

The Cup

In Mediterranean countries, wine is the basic drink, just as bread is the basic food. We can say of wine what we have already said of bread: it is a symbol of unity because it is made from many pressed grapes and because those who eat at the same table share in the same wine. This communion at table is often highlighted by the offering of toasts and by the clinking of glasses as a sign of unity.

We must also recall the supernatural significations of wine. The first of these does not relate directly to wine but to the vine. A number of prophetic texts, especially from Isaias (5:1-7) and Jeremias (2:21), as well as Psalm 80, use the vine or vineyard as a metaphor for the people of God. Israel is the vine which God lovingly tends, which he has even transplanted, but which often disappoints his tender care by yielding more thorns than grapes.

In the Gospel several parables speak of the Kingdom of God as a vineyard into which the owner sends his workers or his sons (Luke 20:9-16; Matthew 20:1-16; 21:28-31). Most important of all, however, in his great discourse at the Supper, Jesus uses the allegory of the vine to describe the people of God, the Church, in its deepest, innermost reality: "I am the true vine. . . . Live on in me, as I do in you. No more than a branch can bear fruit of itself apart from the vine can you bear fruit apart from me" (John 15:1, 4). The vine which yields wine, then, symbolizes throughout the Bible the union of believers in a single people beloved by God, the people who are his Church; and on the evening when he institutes the Eucharist, Jesus chooses the image of the vine in order to bring home to us the need of being completely united to him. All this language and imagery sheds light on the institution of the Eucharist as the sacrament of union with Christ and therefore the sacrament of the Church.

If bread made of crushed grains can call to mind Christ's Passion, wine, which the Bible several times calls the blood of the grape (Gen. 49:11; Deut. 32:14; Sir. 30:15; 1 Macc. 6:34), is even better suited to turn our thoughts to Christ's sacrifice which the Eucharist re-presents and contains. Here, however, we cannot simply present considerations parallel to those we offered concerning the bread, but must strike out along a different path.

MEANING OF THE CUP

You may perhaps have noticed that although the Eucharist consists chiefly of the two consecrations, two different formulas are used for these. Whereas the priest says "This is my body" over the bread he does not say "This is my blood" over the wine, but "This is the cup of my blood." This turn of phrase is backed by reasons which will help us penetrate more deeply into the secrets of the Eucharist.

What, after all, is the value or significance of blood considered directly in itself? Its presence may be due to a serious accident or to a hemorrhage, to a surgical operation or to a crime, to a contribution to a blood bank or to a religious sacrifice. The situation becomes quite clear, however, if the blood is offered to us in a cup or chalice (the two words are synonymous). The cup keeps the blood from spreading around, being lost, and being too elusive to lay hold of. The cup shows that the blood is something precious. Moreover, the cup makes it possible to raise up the blood and offer it to God. Finally, the cup makes it possible to pass the blood around so that each person may drink of it. To speak of the cup of blood is to say that this blood has a religious value, that it is being used in an offering, a sacrifice, and a communion.

This is not simply a gratuitous supposition or an ingenious notion. On several occasions Jesus speaks of a cup in referring to his sacrifice and Passion. When the ambitious mother of James and John naively asks the first place in the Kingdom for her sons, Jesus asks with full seriousness: "Can you drink of the cup I am to drink of?" (Matthew 20:22), meaning "Are you ready to share my suffering before you share my glory?"

In the Garden of Olives we will see Jesus kneeling, his whole human sensibility in revolt, asking his Father: "My Father, if it is possible, let this cup pass me by" (Matthew 26:39). It is clear that he trembles before the vision of the sufferings and abasement of his Passion, and that he must make a heroic effort to accept them. But he did accept them, and when the ever-impetuous Peter, at the moment of Christ's arrest, tried to defend him and cut off Malchus' ear,

Jesus said: "Put your sword back into its sheath. Am I not to drink the cup the Father has given me?" (John 18:11). Here again the cup signifies the Passion as accepted and willed.

Now this is exactly what makes Christ's Passion a sacrifice. Blood symbolizes physical suffering; the cup containing the blood and making it manageable, as it were, represents the loving submission with which the suffering is accepted. The great mystic St. Catherine of Siena uses the following comparison: If a cupbearer must offer a drink to a king, he does not present him with an empty cup; that would be an act of contempt; on the other hand, he cannot offer water without a cup; therefore he combines the water and the cup. The water is suffering, and the cup is love.[1] Suffering that is not accepted with love is worthless in God's sight. Love that is not rested by suffering is likely to be more theoretical than real, and is equivalent to offering God an empty cup. A sacrifice requires the combination of suffering and love, the offering up of blood, under the appearances of wine, in a cup.

THE CUP OF THE COVENANT

Let us turn again to the formula for the consecration of the wine: "this is the cup of my blood, *the blood of the new and everlasting covenant.*" To understand these last words, we must bear in mind the history of Israel. "Covenant," in contemporary French, is the ring symbolizing the union of the wife with her husband, who gave her the ring.[2] Israel, the people of God, was united to God in a very special union, comparable to a marriage. This is why the prophets, when rebuking Israel for her idolatry and disobedience, speak of her as an adulterous wife who is unfaithful to her mysterious spouse, God (cf. especially Hosea 1:1-3; Ezekiel 16). This covenant, anticipated by Noah (Gen. 9:10-17) and Abraham (Gen. 15:18) and concluded by Moses (Exod. 19:24), was always sealed by a sacrifice.

Moses has just received the Law, the Decalogue, from God on Sinai. He reports this to the people, and they declare themselves ready to obey the Law. Then Moses concludes the covenant by immolating bulls, half of whose blood is sprinkled on the people, and half poured out on the altar, which represents God. Then Moses and the elders ascend Mount Sinai, where "they gazed on God. They ate and drank" (Exod. 24:11 — Jerusalem Bible). Such was the former covenant, a pact of union and fidelity between Israel and her God.

Jesus comes to effect a new covenant, a much more intimate union between God and his new people. Like Moses, he begins by promulgating a law, a new law of love and freedom: "I give you a new commandment: Love one another. Such as my love has been for you, so must your love be for each other" (John 13:34). Subsequently he concludes the new covenant by a sacrifice in which blood is shed. But it is no longer the blood of bulls but his own blood, shed in physical reality on the hill of Calvary, and shed sacramentally (that is, in a mysterious yet real way) in the sacrifice of the Eucharist. The words used in the consecration of the wine, "the blood of the new and everlasting covenant," bring us back again to that essential idea which we are always rediscovering as we consider the Eucharist: the Eucharist does not simply effect the union of each soul with God; it also effects the union of all into a single people and a single Church. The Eucharist is the sacrament of unity and of union; the Mass is the sacrifice of the community.

SHARING IN THE CHALICE

The Second Vatican Counsil decided that the laity could once again take Communion from the chalice.[3] This provision has ecumenical significance, since both the Eastern Christians and the Protestants used to be shocked by what seemed to be infidelity to the Gospel. For Jesus says: "If you do not eat the flesh of the Son of Man *and drink his blood*, you have no life in you" (John 6:53). Again, in instituting the Eucharist, he says: "*All of you must drink from it*, for this is my blood" (Matthew 26:29).

The faithful of the Latin Church had taken Communion from the chalice for twelve centuries. The custom fell into disuse during the Middle Ages for a variety of reasons, some theological, others practical. The primary reason seems to have been the general rarity of Communion, which made it almost exclusively a sacrament for the sick; in the case of the sick, however, it was difficult to carry the consecrated wine to them and to have them drink of it.

How can abstention from the chalice be excused? Two doctrinal reasons, still valid, are basic. First of all, Christian faith has always accepted, instinctively but nonetheless surely, that Christ in his entirety — body, blood, soul and divinity — is contained under even the smallest quantity of either of the two Eucharistic species; consequently the believer who receives only under the form of bread receives the whole Eucharist.

Secondly, the priest was rightly regarded as summing up in his person the whole community. It was thought, therefore, that since he at least does, and must, communicate under both forms, Christ's command, "All of you must drink of it," was sufficiently observed.

When, therefore, a present-day believer takes Communion from the chalice, he does not receive any more grace than when he receives only the consecrated bread. As we have indicated, however, wine is naturally a sign of joy. Moreover, Christ's blood reminds us in a more eloquent way of his sacrifice for the forgiveness of the sins of all mankind. Finally, and above all, the cup is the sign "of the new and everlasting covenant," and this is why we have begun once again to give the faithful the chalice when they become members of the Church or enter into a new state of life within the Church, e.g., adult baptism, marriage (what finer sign of union than to drink of the same cup?), religious profession, etc.

The list of occasions on which the faithful may receive from the chalice is steadily being lengthened. If the Church still imposes any limitations in this matter, it is not because she thinks of the chalice as involving some higher kind of Communion that is to be reserved to an elite. The reasons are practical and catechetical: Communion from the chalice should not seem to contradict the doctrine confirmed by the Council of Trent or cause it to be forgotten, namely, that, as regards content, Communion under one form is sufficient and complete. Any superiority, therefore, is only in the order of sign. It is proper, then, that only the faithful who have been instructed in this signification should share the chalice.

[1]St. Catherine of Siena, *Dialogue*, ch. 11.

[2][In French, the word *alliance*, which means "alliance" (match; marriage; union; political alliance] and is the word for the biblical "covenant," also means "wedding ring" — *Translator's note.*]

[3]Cf. *Constitution on the Sacred Liturgy*, no. 55.

[4]The whole teaching and pedagogy of the Instruction of the Sacred Congregation of Rites, *Eucharisticun Mysterium: On the Worship of the Eucharistic Mystery*, May 25, 1967 (cf. *The Pope Speaks*, 12 [1967], pp. 211–236), is dominated by concern for the truth of the signs used.

[5]Cf. *Eucharisticum Mysterium*, no. 32 *(The Pope Speaks, p. 225).*

10.

The Sacrifice

We come now to one of the most difficult points in our study of the Mass. It is clear that the Mass is a meal, since bread and wine are offered and eaten at it. But the Mass is also, and even more essentially, a sacrifice, and this is much less evident. The word "sacrifice" calls up images of an immolated victim and the shedding of blood. Yet, while we see at the celebration of the Mass a table, bread, wine, a plate (the paten), a drinking glass (the chalice), and table linen (the altar cloths), we see neither victim, knife, nor bloodshed. Nonetheless, it is an article of faith that the Mass is a genuine sacrifice. How are we to understand this?

AUTHENTIC CONCEPTION OF SACRIFICE

We will get rid of a good many difficulties if we begin by eliminating some of the incorrect ideas concerning sacrifice. The word, in fact, no longer has any precise meaning for civilized men of the twentieth century; it is used now only in figurative expressions. In such expressions, the term signifies not only something painful but, even more disconcertingly, a loss or privation. We say, for example, that soldiers in

76

battle "sacrifice" their lives. A merchant can speak of selling "at a sacrifice," referring to goods which he knows he cannot make a profit on. We may also read in advertising material that "the management will not stop at any sacrifice to satisfy its customers," that is, it is willing to exert itself and even to accept losses that are good for business. Finally, the children of pious families are invited to make little "sacrifices," all of which take the form of troublesome efforts or privations — getting up early, not resenting a scolding, giving up a delicacy.

Such expressions have accustomed us to look upon a sacrifice as primarily a painful action. The Mass, on the other hand, appears to us as simply a meal (there is nothing painful about that), even a festive meal enhanced by singing, flowers, and lights.

The essential element in a sacrifice, however, is not privation but, on the contrary, enrichment. The purpose of sacrifice, says St. Augustine, is to unite us to God and thus to win for us supreme happiness and enrichment. We seek to obtain this result by performing a visible action which both symbolizes and brings about this union with God. Sacrifice is not carried out in the sphere of spiritual realities but in the sphere of external signs. To offer a sacrifice means to present God with an offering which we are sure he will accept, and it makes of the human, material reality something sacred. To sacrifice means, according to the etymology of the word, "to make (something) sacred." How can we be sure that God will accept and consecrate what we offer him? We are sure because we are not offering him just any gift of our own choice and in a manner we see fit, but the very gift which God has specified and according to the rite he has chosen.

THE MASS, A REAL BUT SACRAMENTAL SACRIFICE

We can now apply these few simple ideas to the
Mass; in doing so we shall begin to understand what a
sacrifice is. The whole of the Mass makes clear to us
that it is a mystery-action addressed to God. Each
individual does not celebrate Mass in his own peculiar
way. It requires an officially appointed person, a
priest, who dresses in distinctive clothing; this fact
already shows us that we are not dealing with a
utilitarian, everyday action. Moreover, the gestures
and words of the priest are not spontaneous but are
regulated by a ceremonial. Not even the offerings are
left to our free determination. They must be bread and
wine because our Lord commanded us to celebrate the
sacrifice by doing what he did when he took bread and
wine at the Last Supper. We lay the offerings on an
altar, that is, not on an ordinary table but on a sacred
table where we are sure of meeting God and of God in
some way coming to accept them. In addition, the
priest *consecrates* the offerings, that is, makes of them
something authentically sacred, since they become the
body and blood of Christ, who is God. Finally, we eat
the bread and drink the wine that have become the
body and blood of Jesus Christ; we cannot more
effectively unite ourselves to God than by taking into
ourselves the divinized humanity of Jesus.

You may object: "But can we really speak of
sacrifice when there is no immolated body, no blood
shed?"

Let us begin our answer by pointing out that in
order to unite ourselves to God — which is the
purpose of sacrifice — we must overcome certain
obstacles. First, there is the obstacle of our egoism: we
always tend to make ourselves the center of the world

and to rebel against God. More particularly, we are separated from God by sin. Such obstacles can be overcome only by the obedience, which makes up for the rebellion of sin, and by the love that breaks through the crust of our egoism. Jesus overcame all these obstacles by his great, unique, and perfect sacrifice of the Cross, for in it his bloody death, accepted in obedient love, repaired the ruin caused by man's sin and egoism. In suffering and dying on the Cross, Jesus offered himself to his Father in a definite and visible way, and thereby reunited to his Father the human race, which had been separated from him by sin. Thus Jesus opened for men the way to happiness. That was the purpose of his sacrifice. Death, blood, and immolation were but means.

Only Jesus, being perfectly pure and holy, could offer this sacrifice. But he wanted us to be able to associate ourselves with it and to offer sacrifice along with him. The sacrifice of Calvary, however, offered as it was once and for all, could not be repeated. But Jesus found a way to truly make this sacrifice present in a different form. On the eve of his death he took bread and wine, consecrated them so that they became his immolated Body and Blood, and commanded us to initiate this mystery-sacrifice over and over again. When we celebrate Mass, we do again what Jesus did at the Last Supper. We do not do again what he did on the Cross. We do not put him to death again, but we render present on the altar the sacrifice of his Body and Blood, in such a way that we renew the offering that redeemed mankind. As is said in the Prayer over the Gifts for the Second Sunday in Ordinary Time: "Every time we celebrate this memorial sacrifice [in every Mass], the work of our redemption [accomplished once and for all on the

Cross] is carried out." Here we have the great mystery of the Mass: it is both a memorial ("Do this in memory of me") and a new bringing about of the work of our redemption.

THE CROSS, THE SUPPER, AND THE MASS

In order better to understand how the Mass, despite its lack of a slaying or other violent action, is nonetheless a sacrifice, let us consider how the Last Supper was a sacrifice. For the Mass, in a literal sense, reproduces the Last Supper and thereby reproduces, though in another language, the Cross itself.

How, then, is the Last Supper a sacrifice? It is a sacrifice, to begin with, because it is a Passover feast. Now the Passover is a sacrifice in the form of a meal. Exodus prescribes that when the Passover meal is repeated and "when your children ask you, 'What does this rite of yours mean?' you shall reply, 'This is the Passover *sacrifice* of the Lord'" (Exod. 12:26).

We can legitimately ask, of course, whether Jesus indeed celebrated the Passover with his disciples, for they ate the Last Supper on Thursday evening. But it seems, if we read St. John, that the Passover was celebrated on Friday evening. He calls Friday itself Preparation Day for the Passover (John 19:14, 31, 42); the Jews were unwilling to enter Pilate's praetorium (or residence) that day "because it was the Preparation Day," and they wanted to be able to eat the Passover. Similarly, the bodies of the crucified men were taken down from the crosses so that they might not remain there during the Sabbath, "since it was [now] Preparation Day."

The synoptic Gospels, however, formally state that the meal of Thursday evening was a Passover meal (Matthew 26:17-19; Mark 14:12, 14, 16; Luke 22:7-8, 11, 13, 15). Nonetheless, they agree with St. John that Friday was the Preparation Day (Matthew 27:62; Mark 15:42; Luke 23:54). We may therefore suppose that the official day of Passover fell that year on Saturday and that the Jews gathered in Jerusalem began the celebration on Friday evening, but that the people from provincial towns, like Jesus and his disciples, who were Galileans, could anticipate the Passover meal on Thursday evening. (Besides, the family from whom Jesus borrowed the dining room needed it themselves to celebrate the Passover meal at the regular time.)

Whatever be the case with this exegetical problem and the quite hypothetical solution just suggested, one thing is sure, and that is the point that interests us: For the synoptic Gospels, which alone report the institution of the Eucharist, the Eucharistic meal is indeed a Passover meal, the true Passover meal. For St. John, the paschal Lamb is the crucified Jesus himself.[1] From these two statements, all the more striking because they are not easy to reconcile, we can deduce the profound identity of Supper and Cross, both of which bring to fulfillment the prefigurative Passover of the former covenant. Whatever the outward rite celebrated at the Supper may have been, it was indeed a Passover, and therefore a sacrifice, like the Cross.

St. John himself relates the Last Supper to the Passover, since he begins his account of events in the supper room with these words: "Before the feast of Passover, Jesus realized that *the hour had come for him to pass from this world to the Father.* He had loved his own in this world, and would show his love for them to the end" (John 13:1). The "hour" of Jesus is St. John's way of expressing the carrying out of the mystery of death and resurrection (John 2:4; 5:25, 28; 12:23, 27; 17:1), while Passover (or "Pasch") means passage (cf. Exod. 12:1).

St. John does not narrate the institution of the Eucharist, but he does report the washing of the feet, the meaning of which is sacrificial. The reasons for this assertion are, first of all, because the action has the same purpose as sacrifice, namely, to effect unity in love; and second, because in washing the feet Jesus adopts the attitude of a servant, thus reminding us of the Suffering Servant (Is. 53) who is put to death for the sins of his people. The parallel we suggest becomes all the more obvious when we read in the Synoptics the discourse that corresponds to John's: "Such is the case with the Son of Man who has come, not to be served by others, but to serve, to give his own life as a ransom for the many" (Matthew 20:28; Mark 10:45; cf. Is. 53:4-12).

The events at the beginning of the Supper are connected with the betrayal by Judas, whom Jesus sends from the supper room so that he may "be quick" about what he is to do. Thus the Supper involves, and in a sense sets in motion, the Passion (John 13:12, 21-30; Matthew 26:21-24; Mark 14:18-21; Luke 22:21-23).

As for the institution of the Eucharist itself, we have already pointed out the sacrificial meaning of the words "This is my body *to be given for you*" (Luke 22:19; 1 Cor. 11:24) and of the whole formula for consecrating the chalice.

The words which follow the washing of the feet in St. John's Gospel (usually called "the discourse in the upper room") also show the sacrificial value of the Eucharist. Not that there is any mention of real presence, immolation, or relation between the Last Supper and the Cross. The general theme, however, is the purpose and fruits of Christ's sacrifice: charity, unity, gathering into a single body. Chapter 17 in particular is rightly called "the priestly [i.e., sacrificial] prayer," and writers have often observed how its style and content remind us strikingly of the very early anaphoras (or liturgical prayer enclosing the consecration).

A final argument, more theological than Scriptural, brings out the deeper unity between the Cross, the Last Supper, and the Mass, and therefore the sacrifical nature of the last two. The Cross is a unique and perfect sacrifice because one and the same Person is both Priest and Victim. Other sacrifices have a priest who may be as conscientious and pious as possible, and a victim which may be as pure and precious as possible; but priest and victim are distinct. The priest offers, but does not offer himself; the victim is immolated, but involuntarily and unknowingly. On the Cross, however, the same Being is both Victim of perfect holiness and Priest who is completely aware of what he is doing.[2] No one can doubt that Jesus is the Victim. And if the Cross is not just a news item, not just the result of a judicial error, but a genuine sacrifice, then Jesus, so perfectly master of his own situation, is its Priest.[3]

On the Cross, Jesus is Priest and Victim in his own person, in his natural, physical state. At the Last Supper, too, he is Priest and Victim, but though he is Priest directly in his own person, he is Victim in a sacramental way, under the outward forms of bread and wine (so that he is immolated and his blood is shed only in a sacramental way). Finally, in the Mass, Jesus is once again Priest and Victim. He is Victim in a sacramental way, just as at the Last Supper, but here he is also Priest in a sacramental way, inasmuch as the consecratory words are pronounced by a human priest who takes his place.

All these considerations show that the immolation of the Mass is a genuine but *re-presentative* immolation. In other words, it is *sacramental,* inasmuch as the Mass reproduces the Last Supper, which in turn re-presented and involved the Cross in its entirety.

WHY RENEW THE ONE SACRIFICE?

The Mass, then, translates into sacramental language the redemptive reality contained in the Cross and makes possible its renewal. But to what purpose? Did not Christ's once-and-for-all sacrifice on the Cross suffice to save the world? Of course! But Christ wanted us to cooperate in our own salvation. He did not want us to be saved without contributing anything. Therefore he gave us the Eucharist to make it possible for us to offer *our* sacrifice in union with *his* sacrifice. Our offering of the consecrated bread and wine is not intended solely for renewing the sacrifice of Christ, but also for uniting our own sacrifice to his. As St. Augustine put it, God who created us without our help has not willed to save us without our help. This is why the Church does not wish us simply to be present at Mass, as though it were a sacrifice going on at a distance, with us there only as spectators and passive beneficiaries, she asks us to participate in the sacrifice, to unite ourselves to it, to offer ourselves with Christ, and to incorporate ourselves into him through Communion. If it were otherwise, there would be no need to go to Mass; in fact, the celebration of the Mass would be useless. It would be enough for Christians to recall occasionally that once, a long time ago, Jesus died for them, and to let themselves be saved without doing anything on their own.

OUR SACRIFICE

Does offering ourselves with Christ and immolating ourselves with him mean that we too ought to climb Calvary and shed our blood there? No, of course not. It means that we should participate in the Mass in an intelligent, active way; that we ought to try to understand what the priest is doing and to manifest our union with him and among ourselves by our responses, songs, and outward attitudes. It means, above all, that we should not be content to be present at Mass as at a ceremony which has no influence on our lives. Rather, we should derive a resoluteness from it; we should derive the strength to do away with all that blocks our union with God and to develop all that deepens this union, that is, first and foremost, our loving dedication to God and our brothers. The Mass or Eucharist is the sacrament of sacrifice, which means, finally, the sacrament of our divinization through the generous gift of ourselves.

The simplest and most effective way to understand both the meaning of this sacrifice in itself and for human living is to keep in mind its purpose: *atonement for sin.* This sacrifice did away with the guilt of sin before God. Sharing in Calvary's sacrifice (the Mass) means sharing in forgiveness of sin and the guilt due to sin. To continue in personal sin undoes the work of the Cross, nullifies the sacrifice of Christ, and makes the Mass useless. All the other ways of participation in Mass — singing, reading, listening, answering responses, kneeling, standing, sitting — are so much hypocrisy for the individual who clings to his sinful ways. On the other hand, perfect participation is realized by the repentant sinner who allows himself to be washed clean in the sacrificial blood of the Lamb, and then goes "and sins no more."

[1] Cf. John 19:33-36, "When they came to Jesus and saw that he was already dead, they did not break his legs. . . . These events took place for the fulfillment of Scripture: 'Break none of his bones.'" The quoted words are a ritual prescription for the Passover meal (Exod. 12:46).

[2] The new Eucharistic Prayers highlight this point: "Before he was given up to death, a death he freely accepted . . ." (Second Prayer); "In fulfillment of your will he gave himself up to death" (Fourth Prayer).

[3] The point could be the subject of a lengthy development. Observe how Jesus does not simply let himself be taken but gives his life freely (John 10:17); how he freely goes up to Jerusalem, although he knows what awaits him; how he identifies himself and presents himself to those who have come to arrest him; how his answer to Caiaphas goes beyond the question asked and will bring about his condemnation; how he keeps silent or speaks with authority before Herod and Pilate; how he speaks on the Cross, without complaint and as one who is master of the situation, etc. All of this is confirmed by the fact that he raises himself up as he had foretold (John 10:18).

11.

The Resurrection of Christ

The Eucharist is clearly the memorial of the Lord's death. We must not forget, however, that it is at the same time the sacrament of the resurrection. This statement points to two distinct but connected facts, both of them very important. First, the Christ present in the Eucharist is the risen Christ; second, we receive the Eucharist as a pledge of our own resurrection.

CHRIST PRESENT IN THE EUCHARIST IS THE RISEN CHRIST

First, then, the Christ present in the Eucharist is the risen Christ. We cannot, in fact, separate Christ's death from his resurrection. By dying for us, Christ proved his love for us. Yet his death would have been fruitless had it not been followed by his resurrection. Recall how dejected the apostles were — they had seen Christ die, but they did not believe that he would rise again. Recall the discouragement of the men on the road to Emmaus — they had seen all their hopes come crashing down in the painful death on Calvary. Some years later St. Paul would say: "If Christ was not raised . . . if our hopes in Christ are limited to this life only, we are the most pitiable of men" (1 Cor. 15:17, 19). Christ's death, without his ensuing resurrection, was only a terrible defeat, undergone against his will; his death followed by his resurrection was a voluntary sacrifice and a victory.

We must not think of the resurrection as though it were a kind of unimportant afterthought, a kind of guarantee that the Passion had not been useless. Many Christians today see Good Friday as being more important than Easter. The first apostles did not think so. The great theme of their preaching was the triumphant cry: "Christ is risen!" This, of course, implies that he had first died. But the two mysteries of death and resurrection are in reality only one; they make up the basic mystery of Christianity: the paschal mystery. St. John tells us that on Holy Thursday Jesus knew that the moment had come for him to *pass* from this world to his Father. The paschal mystery consists precisely in this *passage*, for "Pasch" means "passage."

Every passage, however, supposes a point of departure and a point of arrival. In Christ's passage or Pasch, the point of departure is the death by which he painfully left this world; the point of arrival is his resurrection, which, completed by his ascension, assures his glorious return to the Father. The mystery of our salvation is this same mystery of the Pasch, with its two distinguishable but inseparable faces: the humilitating, painful, purifying face of suffering and death; and the glorious, joyful, fruitful face of resurrection. The Eucharist contains the whole mystery of our salvation and puts it daily at our disposal. It contains the mystery in a concrete, here-and-now way, for it contains the very Person of Christ. Therefore the Christ who is present in the Eucharist is the Christ who died and then rose from the dead.

One objection comes immediately to mind. The words of consecration, which effect the real presence of Christ in the Eucharist, do not refer at all to his resurrection and seem to envisage only his Passion and death, inasmuch as they refer successively to his body and his blood. For the separation of body and blood can be predicated only of a being subjected to a violent death.

Two answers may be given to this objection. We can repeat what we said above: the death of Christ cannot really be separated from his resurrection, for if the Eucharist presented us with only the dead Christ, it would not contain the whole mystery of our salvation.

There is another answer which goes more directly to the point. The consecration renders the body and blood of Christ present in the Eucharist as they are in their objective reality at the present moment. The celebrant speaks in the present tense: "This *is* my body. . . . This *is* the cup of my blood." It is admittedly the case that the words Jesus himself spoke did not have to contain the verb "is"; he probably said: "This my body. . . . This my blood." But the biblical text and the liturgical formulas used ever since do contain the verb "is." More importantly, there is question of an action in the present: "Take, eat," words which refer to the consecrated elements which we do eat here and now.

In other words, we do not have a historical, symbolic, or commemorative statement but a present action. But at the present moment Christ is in heaven — risen, living, glorious. The words of consecration must, therefore, make the risen, living, glorious Christ present in the Eucharist. The words do, of course, refer to and produce directly either the body alone or the blood alone. But the body is a living body and, in becoming present under the form of bread, brings the blood with it. The very fact that for centuries the faithful in the West received only the body of Christ in Communion shows that the Christ who is present in the Eucharist is the living, risen Christ.

There are some further proofs to be drawn from the liturgy. Immediately after the consecration, the priest says a very important and very beautiful prayer — the *anamnesis,* or prayer of remembrance, found in all the liturgies. When the priest has repeated Christ's words: "Do this in memory of me," the congregation sings an acclamation which links the death, resurrection, and return of Christ.[1] Then the priest continues: "Father, we celebrate the memory of Christ, your Son. We, your people and your ministers, recall his passion, his resurrection from the dead, and his ascension into glory; and from the many gifts you have given us we offer to you, God of glory and majesty, this holy and perfect sacrifice." Thus the Roman Canon (First Eucharistic Prayer). The Second Eucharistic Prayer is briefer: "In memory of his death and resurrection, we offer you, Father, this life-giving bread, this saving cup." The two other Eucharistic Prayers have anamneses with the same structure: *remembering* his death and resurrection, *we offer you* (present tense).

If we believe these formulas, each Mass renders present on the altar not only the Passion of Christ but all his mysteries. This is why the Church can celebrate feasts of every kind by offering the Mass and repeating the Eucharistic consecration. Whether it is Easter or Christmas or Ascension, we always celebrate the Mass, because the Mass contains Christ living in his total mystery, in which he keeps the glorious marks of his death. The celebration of Mass throughout the Church year and on all its various feasts is a further proof that the Eucharist renders the living, risen Christ present to us. Let us not forget, moreover, that the first of these feasts — first in importance no less than in date of origin — is the feast of the Pasch, the feast of the dead and now risen Christ. The first Christians, it seems, knew no other feast, and the Pasch is still today the "solemnity of solemnities." Only gradually did special feasts such as Christmas and the Ascension come into existence. The primary object of our faith, the center and high point of the New Covenant mystery, is always Christ who died and is now risen.

After breaking the bread, the priest drops a fragment of his host into the chalice. We do not know the exact origin of this action. But we may be allowed to see in this reunion of the body and blood of Christ a sign recalling that the Christ present and immolated on the altar is, after all, the living, risen Christ, even though the separate consecration of the body and blood had signified his death.

It is evident that certain ideas which some people may have of the Eucharist need revision. Our religion is not first and foremost a religion of remembrance and of the past. It is a religion of life, hope, and conquest, a religion directed to life and resurrection. The Eucharist, the center and sun of our Catholicism, is not and cannot be the sacrament of death and bloody sacrifice taken in utter isolation. Death and sacrifice are means; they are paths that must be trodden, but they lead to the radiant glory of resurrection. The way to the empty tomb begins at Calvary's Cross.

[1]The allusion to 1 Corinthians 11:26 is common to the various acclamations.

12.

Our Resurrection

THE EUCHARIST GIVES ETERNAL LIFE

If the Eucharist contains the risen Christ and is the sacrament of Pasch or passage, then its effect must be to make risen men of us too. The Eucharist, after all, assimilates us to Christ. We have here a general law: All nutrition involves assimilation. Ordinary foods are assimilated to the eater, so that in eating I bestow upon the steer or the lettuce the honor of becoming part of my human body's substance; the inferior being is always assimilated to the superior. In the Eucharist, however, he who eats is assimilated to him who is eaten. St. Augustine expresses the point concisely when he puts into Christ's mouth the words: "I am the food of the strong; eat me, and you will be changed into me, not I into you." By eating the risen Christ, we must ourselves become risen men in his image and under his direct influence.

Jesus himself tells us this in the great discourse on the bread of life which he spoke after the multiplication of the loaves in order to pave the way for the institution of the Eucharist. "Let me firmly assure you, he who believes has eternal life. I am the bread of life. Your ancestors ate manna in the desert, but they died. This is the bread that comes down from heaven for a man to eat and never die. I myself am the living bread come down from heaven. If anyone eats this bread he shall live forever; the bread I will give is my flesh, for the life of the world" (John 6:47-51). A little further on, he repeats the same thoughts in an even more forceful and pointed way: "Let me solemnly assure you, if you do not eat the flesh of the Son of Man and drink his blood, you have no life in you. He who feeds on my flesh and drinks my blood has life eternal, and I will raise him up on the last day. . . . This is the bread that came down from heaven. Unlike your ancestors who ate and died nonetheless, the man who feeds on this bread shall live forever" (John 6:53-54, 58).

The reason for this startling claim? "For my flesh is real food and my blood real drink. The man who feeds on my flesh and drinks my blood remains in me, and I in him. Just as the Father who has life sent me and I have life because of the Father, so the man who feeds on me will have life because of me" (John 6:55-57).

The reasoning is quite simple. Christ's body is genuine food. The purpose of food is to give life. Christ's life, however, is a divine life, the very life of the heavenly Father. Consequently, in taking in this true food which Christ's body is, we are united to his life, which is God's life, eternal life.

We see here with what a keen and virile spirit the Catholic should go to Mass to find there courage, consolation, and strength against temptation and, in general, against all the affliction, all the wear and tear which life has in store for us. We do not go to Mass to have our hearts touched in a more or less sensible way; we go because there we enter into a mysterious but

fully real communion with the life of Christ, with that
divine life which flows into us and becomes our own
life.

HOLY VIATICUM

The Catholic Church has an ancient practice, one
too neglected these days, which brilliantly highlights
the significance of the Eucharist as the sacrament of
eternal life and resurrection. That practice is Holy
Viaticum.[1] The word signifies Communion
administered to a dying person. But we have mean-
while gotten into the habit of thinking of last
anointing as the sacrament of the dying; the
postconciliar reform brings out very clearly that the
sacrament of anointing is for the sick, and that indeed
is its proper name.[2]

There is, however, a sacrament for the dying,
whether they are medically ill or not; that sacrament is
the Eucharist given as *Viaticum*, a word which means
"provisions for a journey." As he is about to make the
great journey and pass into immortality, the Christian
should take with him "the holy and very necessary
Viaticum," as earlier Christians called it. Reception of
Viaticum by the dying is an obligation. For this reason
many of the usual regulations are set aside at this
time. A person who has already communicated may
and should receive Viaticum on the same day. A priest
may and should celebrate Mass, for the second time if
need be, should that be required in order to provide a
dying person with Viaticum. So strong was the belief
of certain early Christians in the efficacy of Viaticum
that we find the abusive practice of giving
Communion even to the dead. All these various facts
show the extent to which the Eucharist is the sacra-

ment of immortaility not only for the soul but even for the body. For the body too must rise on the last day, just as Christ arose, the Christ whose life-giving flesh the Christian has been eating throughout his mortal life.

I spoke of rising on the last day. The Eucharist is the sacrament of our resurrection and makes risen men of us, but we are well aware that we do not rise bodily now. We are risen in grace and in hope. We should not think of this hope, however, as being only a vague probability. It is certain because Christ, our Head, whose members we are, is already risen. St. Paul could therefore say with bold trust: "Both with and in Christ Jesus he [God] raised us up and gave us a place in the heavens" (Eph. 2:6). By reason of our baptism, our resurrection is already assured.

When the priest receives a person seeking baptism at the door of the church, he asks the following questions: "What do you ask of the Church of God? — Faith (i.e., baptism, which is the sacrament of faith). — What does faith give you? — Eternal life." The priest does not speak of the future: "What *will* it give you?" but of the present: "What *does* it give you?" Christ said: "Whoever believes in the Son *has* life eternal" (John 3:36; cf. 5:24).

THE SACRAMENT OF PROGRESS

Risen life, eternal life, is already ours through baptism, because baptism incorporates us into the dead and now risen Christ. But we must still win that eternal life by means of our daily living. Here is where the Eucharist has its place. The Eucharist is a sacrament which requires something more than a reverent or even pious reception; it requires a determination to grow in Christian life, to make progress in the love of God and of our brothers. Children eat in order to grow; adults, admittedly, keep on eating only in order to recoup their energies. Spiritually, however, we are children as long as we are on earth, and we will reach adulthood only in heaven. As long as we live on earth, we must continue to grow and advance.

The sacrament of this continuing progress is the Eucharist. The other sacraments are given but once, or at least are repeated only in certain limited circumstances: when we have sinned, when we are ill, when we enter marriage. But the Eucharist is our daily bread, the sacrament we must receive continually. The criterion which should determine the frequency of our Communions is not our pleasure, for the Eucharist is not a spiritual delicacy. The criterion is not the perfection we have reached, for the Eucharist is not a reward. The criterion is our desire and, above all, our need to grow in strength, in virtue, and most especially in that which is the source of all the virtues — love. The Eucharist, then, is a sacrament which turns our gaze upward and onward. It is not meant for us if we have decided to advance no farther.

The Prayers after Communion (the "post-communion" prayers) usually follow this pattern: Lord, we have shared in your mysteries, we have received your body. Let that not be for us a mere outward rite; let it transform our lives, so that, ever progressing, we may reach the heaven of which this sacrament of your dead and risen body gives not simply the promise but the foretaste and the beginning.

[1]Cf. L. Beauduin, "Le Viatique," *Maison-Dieu*, no. 15 (3rd quarter, 1948), pp. 117–129.
[2]Cf. *Constitution on the Sacred Liturgy*, no. 75.

13.

The Memorial of the Future

THE RETURN OF CHRIST

The Christian is not a man of the past but of the future. He is one who is waiting, wholly turned to the future world. Christians of today have unfortunately forgotten this essential dimension of their faith, yet they continue to recite each Sunday the Nicene Creed, in which the future has such an important place! In the Creed we proclaim our faith in Christ, who was not only born of the Virgin Mary and suffered under Pontius Pilate (two events of the past, part of the historical continuum) but also, once risen, "ascended into heaven and is seated at the right hand of the Father. He will come again in glory to judge the living and the dead."

In the third part of the Creed, after professing our faith in Christ as Judge at the end of time, we also profess our faith in the Holy Spirit and his work — the life of the Church, whose vital principle he is. The Creed ends with this extraordinary double affirmation concerning the goal and apotheosis of the Church's life in the Spirit: "We look for the resurrection of the dead, and the life of the world to come. Amen."

In the Gospels the belief in Christ's return and in

the world to come constantly finds expression. Chapters 24 and 25 of St. Matthew are wholly given over to it. There we find the parable of the servants. Some of them fall asleep, but others keep vigil while their master is off on a journey. Some, therefore, are taken by surprise at his unexpected return in the night like a thief, but the others give him a joyous welcome. There is also the parable of the virgins, another prediction of the Last Judgment, when the Son of Man, Spouse of the Church, will come upon the clouds, as the prophets, especially Daniel (7:13-14), had foretold, and as Jesus himself solemnly affirmed before Caiaphas. In fact, we may say that he died because he claimed to be the supreme Judge at the end of time (Matthew 26:64).

In the sermons and letters of the apostles, we find the same constant preoccupation. The Second Letter of St. Peter and the two Letters of St. Paul to the Thessalonians — especially the second — deal with popular errors concerning the imminence of Christ's coming. They put the faithful on guard against an interpretation of the coming which would render them passive and lead to a kind of fatalism or quietism. But these same letters do not therefore insist any the less on the ontological, if not chronological, proximity of Christ's return and on the duty of actively awaiting it, preparing for it, and hastening it. The apostles constantly refer to the "Day of the Lord," thus taking up and Christianizing a phrase from the prophets and psalms which refers to the terrible judgment which the Lord of the universe will exercise.

The great prayer of the early Christians was: "Come, Lord Jesus!" (Aramaic: *Maran atha*); it concludes not only the First Letter to the Corinthians but the Apocalypse as well, and thus the Bible as a whole.

THE PRAYER OF REMEMBRANCE, OR ANAMNESIS

If the expectation of the Day of the Lord, and the eschatological element generally, is essential to our faith and our life, how could it be absent from the Mass? Yet the Mass is the "memorial" of the Lord, and when we speak of "memorial" and "remembering," we seem to be turning back to the past. Has our Mass no other purpose than to awaken in us the remembrance of Jesus' benefactions? No, the Mass is not a memorial pure and simple, a mere sign which can only stir our memory and stimulate our devotion. The Mass possesses, rather, a quite different kind of realism; its rich content is of quite a different order. When we say that the words of consecration effect the "real presence," we must give their full meaning to these last words and not make them refer simply to a somewhat restricted, static presence of the person of Jesus under the forms of bread and wine. We are speaking of a *presence,* that is, a here-and-now reality in the *present,* and of a *real* presence, that is, the presence of the whole reality of the mysteries of Christ as he lives in his Church and gives life to her. This fuller meaning, which we shall be discussing, is not contrary to the current sense given to the expression "real presence," but, on the contrary, brings out its momentous implications.

It was sometimes customary, in days gone by, to sing a motet to the Blessed Sacrament after the consecration. But this practice meant mistakenly adopting a limited interpretation of "real presence," whereas the liturgical prayers which were being recited after the consecration were inspired by quite different views and opened up quite different perspectives.

At the end of the consecration of the chalice, the priest repeats the words of Jesus: "Do this in memory of me." The Greek word for "memory" in the Gospels is *anamnesis*, which supplies the name for the prayer immediately following the consecration.

In effect, the people by their acclamation and the priest by his prayer of anamnesis are responding to Christ's command by affirming their belief in the presence, mediated through the consecrated bread and wine, of all the mysteries of Christ, for the Eucharist contains and recapitulates them all.

Let us consider the three principal mysteries mentioned in the *anamnesis* and try to understand how they contain the future.

1) The *blessed Passion* (the Latin text contains the untranslated adjective) is the dawn of the new age, the beginning of the last times. It ends the age of sin and opens up the age of holiness. The holy Church — the new human race and the new Jerusalem — is born from the opened side of Jesus from which blood and water flow, "leaping up to provide eternal life" (John 4:14). Now men have in their possession this treasure of holiness, which is more than enough to save all men. Now heaven is open, not only because the obstacles which barred entry to it have been removed, but also, and more positively, because mankind has nothing more to do, until the end of the world and even into heaven, than to draw upon the inexhaustible capital which is the sacrifice of Jesus.

One historical episode from the Passion is quite significant here. On the Cross, Jesus addresses the repentant thief: "I assure you: this day you will be with me in paradise" (Luke 23:43). The question has been asked: What does "this day" mean? Is the thief to be in paradise before Jesus, who will not enter there for forty days, at his ascension? The problem is a false one. The words "this day" do not signify a period of twenty-four hours. We are dealing here, not with earthly chronology, but with the economy of salvation. "This day" is the day of the Lord that begins with his blessed Passion; it is that day that follows upon the long vigil of preparation and expectation which is the former covenant, and will be climaxed by the judgment when the Lord's day will coincide with eternity. Jesus is replying to the prayer of the thief: "Jesus, remember me when you enter upon your reign." He is telling the man that between his own crucifixion and return there is no real interval, despite appearances.

2) The *resurrection* is not merely an event in the personal life of Jesus. Since he is the head of the human race and the first-born of many brothers, his resurrection marks the beginning of ours, which will not be fully a reality until the "resurrection of the body" on the day of the Lord's coming and judgment. Such is the argument that supports the reasoning of St. Paul in 1 Corinthians 15: If Christ is risen, then we shall all rise, because our resurrection is contained in his. That is why he rose on the first day of the week, which is also the eighth day — because his resurrection is the beginning of a new created order, a new world that follows upon and replaces the old. The permanent order of things replaces the temporary order.

The anamnesis prayers also speak of Jesus' descent into the abode of the dead (Fourth Eucharistic Prayer) and of his resurrection from there (First Eucharistic Prayer, or Roman Canon). The mention is important. Jesus rises after having reached the very depths of human wretchedness and, at the same time, the mysterious depths in which the just men of the former covenant were waiting for him. He went to throw open the doors and empty out their "prison" (1 Peter 3:19), for the time of waiting in captivity is over.

3) Jesus definitively eliminated this captivity by his *ascension into glory.* "Thus you find Scripture saying: 'When he ascended on high, he took a host of captives and gave gifts to men.' 'He ascended'— what does this mean but that he had first descended into the lower regions of the earth? He who descended is the very one who ascended high above the heavens, that he might fill all men with his gifts" (Eph. 4:8-10, quoting Ps. 68:19). The ascension, through which the humanity of Jesus begins its glorious reign at the right hand of the Father and introduces our humanity into heaven, already looks forward to Christ's glorious return as Judge of the universe. Thus the angels could say to the apostles: "Men of Galilee, why do you stand there looking up at the skies? This Jesus who has been taken from you will return, just as you saw him go up into the heavens" (Acts 1:11).

Other liturgies, less reserved than our Roman rite, have extended the enumeration in the anamnesis, adding, for example, a mention of the parousia, or glorious coming of Christ at the of time. As a matter of fact, the three mysteries of our anamnesis imply the parousia. For in "remembering" the Passion, resurrection, and ascension, the Eucharist renders present in sacramental form the mysteries of the world to come. Thereby, it prepares for, and is a beginning of, a future world in which it will itself have no place, for that future world will be one of absolute reality. Not only the empty figures of the Old Covenant but even the sacramental signs (however reality-filled) of the New Covenant — will disappear, along with faith and hope. St. Paul puts it briefly: "Every time . . . you eat this bread and drink this cup, you proclaim the death of the Lord *until he comes!*" (1 Cor. 11:26).

The returning Christ, by beginning the order of unveiled reality, of face-to-face vision and unmediated union, will abolish the Eucharist, not of course in regard to the reality the Eucharist contains but in regard to the sacramental signs. There will be no more Pasch or passage, because the goal will have been reached and possessed. The manna prefigured the present order of things, for it fell each day during the crossing of the desert, which symbolized the unfolding of our lives as pilgrims on earth. The manna ceased to fall when the promised land was reached. The natural fertility of the latter made this giving of daily bread no longer necessary; the Chosen People now lived under the sign of an eternal today and of total possession.

PERSPECTIVES ON THE FUTURE

Further details are added to the anamnesis and its anticipation of glory in the two prayers which follow in the Roman Canon.

The prayer "Look with favor" *(Supra quae)* links up the Eucharistic sacrifice with the sacrifices offered during the time of promise. Abel prefigures Christ because Abel is the just man who offers God an acceptable sacrifice and completes it in his own blood, shed in a criminal act by his brother. Abraham prefigures the Father who gives his Son to death. (As the Preface for the Consecration of an Altar in the French ritual puts it: "The Son is offered, the Lamb is slain.") Abraham's sacrifice pre-figures ours as well, for it is acceptable to God by reason of the faith and obedience that inspired it. Finally, Melchizedek, a "priest of God Most High" (Gen. 14:18), that is, of the transcendent God, offers bread and wine, and thus prefigures the priesthood of Christ; Christ is therefore said to be "a priest forever, according to the order of Melchizedek" (Heb. 5:6; cf. Gen. 14:18-20; Ps. 110:4).

Undoubtedly all these prefigurative sacrifices have little substantial value in comparison with the Eucharist. What keeps the comparison from being wholly unsuitable is that Christ's sacrifice, which has no like if considered in itself, has become *our* sacrifice in the Mass. The comparison with the old sacrifices has to do primarily with the sentiments which inspired Abel, Abraham, and Melchizedek, and which ought to inspire us. A sacrifice derives its value not solely from the victim offered but from the intentions of the offerers as well. If those just men of old were inspired by faith and religious devotion, was this not because they hoped for the age to come? Were their sacrifices not a presaging of the only true sacrifice, and did they not participate in its holiness in advance?

The prayer "Almighty God, we pray" *(Supplices)* looks only to the future. It connects the sacrifice being offered at this altar (a term left vague; the altar is both the unique altar of the Cross and the many altars of our churches) with the eternal sacrifice being offered on the heavenly altar, a term which, says St. Thomas, means God himself.[1] The same theologian notes that there is no question of "carrying aloft" the Eucharistic gifts in the sense of material gifts under the forms of bread and wine. What is to borne to heaven is ourselves, the Mystical Body, for that too is mysteriously present in the gifts, although in a different way. Thus the Eucharistic sacrifice, if we take it in the most inclusive way, attains the goal of redemption and the whole plan of salvation — our transfer into the possession of God, our reunion with him in one body so that we, each and all, may be "filled with every grace and blessing." That petition is to be fulfilled in a moment through Communion, the "pledge of heavenly glory" and foretaste of heaven.

The Mass is thus a daily sacrifice, taking place here and now; it is as real and as concrete each day as the new host placed on the paten, and the wine, different today than yesterday, that is poured into the chalice. Each daily Mass is as unique and fresh and new as the day's new dawn, as the day's unfolding flower. But the reality is a sacramental one: it speaks of, and points to, something other than itself. It carries us back to the past, to the mysteries of the historical Christ in which it itself has its roots and from which it derives all its realism and all its divine life-giving power. At the same time, it involves, foretells, and guarantees fruitfulness for a future in which it will finally vanish, as the dawn is absorbed by the sun or as the flower sheds its petals in order to bear fruit. Such is the complex mystery to which we have given the paradoxical title which the reader perhaps now understands: the memorial of the future.

[1]St. Thomas Aquinas, *Summa theologiae*, III, q. 83, a. 4, ad 9.

14.

From Mass to Mass

If we are to fully understand the eschatological value of the Mass, we must not restrict ourselves to considering the mystery of the Mass in itself, as if it were completely fulfilled once and for all on a single occasion. The Cross is indeed unique: Christ died once and for all, and his sacrifice is perfect enough to save the whole world. The Last Supper, too, is unique: it was the institution of a rite. But the rite was instituted in order that it might be repeated. When the rite is one of initiation, such as baptism, it can be done but once for any given individual. This point emerges even more clearly if we think of what baptism accomplishes; death, resurrection, and rebirth are acts that cannot be repeated for the same individual. If, then, the Church does repeat them until the end of time, it does so in order that all who came into the world may, one after the other, be brought into her fold. When we come to the Mass, however, the rite in which the Lord's sacrifice is carried out is a meal, a feeding, an action whose very nature demands that it be repeated frequently and without limitation. The Eucharist is a daily bread, and the Lord gives it to us each day. Consequently we cannot obtain a complete idea of the Mass and its power unless we consider Masses as succeeding one another in time.

MASS: SUNDAY, EASTER, AND VIGIL

The repetition of the Mass, which at first was not celebrated daily, is bound up with the weekly recurrence of "the Lord's day," which was instituted by Jesus himself. It was on the first day of the week, the day after the Sabbath (Matthew 28:1; Luke 24:1; John 20:19) that he appeared to his apostles in his risen body and shared their meal. He then disappeared for a whole week. His second apparition occurred "a week later," again in the context of a meal (John 20:26).

Thus the first "return of the Lord" took place on the first day of the week, which soon came to be called "the Lord's day." It occurred during a fraternal meal, perhaps in the same upper room where Jesus had instituted the Eucharist and spoken at length of his departure and return. In their intense expectation of their Lord's final coming, the apostles may have thought that his final return, like his first one, would take place at daybreak on Sunday, that is, at the same hour and on the same day as the resurrection. But Jesus had told them to "keep vigil" so that they might be ready when he came. The celebration of Sunday, therefore, began at evening on the day before (for people of this time, the day began at sundown). The celebration undoubtedly included, first of all, the Jewish ceremonial ritual of the *lucernarium*, or "lighting of the lamps." The night was spent in praying, singing, and listening to the word of God and the homilies of the apostles. These songs, prayers, and sermons were not meant simply to pass the time and ward off sleep; rather, they opened the hearts of the participants and fostered the "watchfulness" of faith and hope. Our Liturgy of the Word and, in part, our office of praise, the Liturgy of the Hours, derive from this vigil that was filled with prayer and God's word.

At dawn the meeting came to its climax in the "breaking of the bread," the sacrament of love. In this way, even though the Lord did not return in his visible person, the expectation was not disappointed. The prayer *Maran atha* was answered in its twofold meaning: "Come, Lord!" and "The Lord has come." Those present had waited, they were still waiting, yet their longing had already been fulfilled. In the morning each returned to his own occupation, strengthened now to await in a more perfect way the full return of the Lord which had been prefigured and anticipated in the "Lord's Supper." "Supper" too had a twofold meaning: it not only prefigured the supper at which the Lord would come in his visible person, as he had on Easter morning, and sit down among his disciples; the supper was also the meal which Christ had instituted and prepared, the meal in which he gave himself as food, as he had done on Holy Thursday evening.

The Roman liturgy does not seem to have preserved this vigil as such, or at least does not seem to have celebrated it weekly. But the "weekly Passover" was soon to give rise to the "annual Passover," and, in connection with the latter, the holy vigil, "mother of all vigils," would be observed for centuries. It then fell into disuse as the eschatological sense faded and was reinstated by an inspired and providential act of Pope Pius XII at Easter, 1951.

THE MYSTERY OF THE LITURGICAL YEAR

The institution of the annual Passover marks the first step in creating the liturgical year. The mystery-reality of this year wholly eludes us if we fail to bear in mind the mystery of the Eucharistic anamnesis. The latter renders present the entire mystery of Christ in a very real but global way. But the Church, which lives in time and is a people on pilgrimage toward the world to come, needs to spell out this global mystery in detail. In does so by means of the liturgical seasons and feasts. Without the presence of the Eucharist, the seasons and feasts would be only a series of more or less dramatic representations; they would undoubtedly have great pedagogical value, but their only reality would be in the minds of the faithful. It is the Eucharist that gives all these reminders of the past their full reality and relevance to us, all the more so since the glorious Christ, present in the Eucharist, sums up in himself all his earlier mysteries, for the latter were not canceled out, as it were, by those that followed. A man can achieve manhood only if he "put[s] childish ways aside" (1 Cor. 13:11); but when Christ became a grown man, the mysteries and states of his childhood did not simply vanish, any more than his resurrection caused the mysteries and states of his toil-filled years of manhood and of his Passion simply to disappear. (The "marks" on the body of the risen Christ point to this aspect of the mystery of Christ.) For this reason the Christian who meditates on the mysteries of the rosary can make his own the joyful and sorrowful mysteries, even though Christ is now, and has long been, in his glory.

The liturgical "mysteries," on the contrary, are celebrated by the Church on determined days. Why are there such set dates for each mystery? The reason is simply that the Church, entrusted with the mystery of her Spouse, celebrates them on those dates. The ultimate ground of the reality of the liturgical year is the mystery of the incarnate Word. But the reason why the year has come into existence is the twofold but inseparable mystery of the Eucharist and the Church. Every time the Church celebrates a feast, she insists on the "today": "Today" Jesus is born, or is risen, or sends his Spirit upon the apostles. The contemporaneity of each mystery is due to the realism of the Eucharistic celebration and to the power which the Church, gathered for the occasion, has received of celebrating, applying, and profiting by the priestly work of her Spouse.

Liturgical feasts, then, are far more than commemorations and reminders of the past. Nonetheless, even if they are, as we have just maintained, celebrations of a present mystery, how are we to explain the constant repetition of them? What is the point of constantly starting anew an enclosed cycle?

As a matter of fact, the cycle is not closed. To pursue the geometric comparison: the cycle is like a spiral rather than a circle. Each feast represents progress in relation to the same feast as celebrated in the preceding year, for it brings the return of Christ closer to us and advances us toward the great unending feast of the world to come. In other words, the liturgical cycle, and each feast and season in it, is eschatological.

Advent, therefore, is not intended — in the objective order of things — to prepare our souls for Christmas. We know perfectly well that Jesus was born at Bethlehem a long time ago, and we cannot imitate the expectation of the patriarchs. His coming at Christmas and his epiphany are a pledge and prefiguration of his final coming, and it is for the latter that Advent prepares us, as the prayers and readings of the season prove.

Again, during Lent, do we really await the resurrection of Christ? Not at all. The resurrection occurred centuries ago. Rather, in making the resurrection real and operative for us through the celebration or renewal of our baptism, we are looking forward to the return of Christ; his resurrection was a first step in that coming and a pledge of it. If you have trouble accepting this idea, then carefully re-read the liturgy for Palm Sunday. It shows that what we celebrate that day is not simply the memory of our Lord's momentary triumph, but also the expectation of his return and of our entrance after him into heaven, where we will be received by the angels, whom the Hebrew children with their "hosannas" prefigured.

The season after Pentecost is eschatological through and through. It portrays the growth of the Church, under the inspiration of the Holy Spirit, from the time when her Spouse vanished from her sight until his return, of which she is reminded by Advent and the beginning of a new cycle.

From feast to feast, from Mass to Mass, the Church becomes holier and more deeply imbued with the Spirit of Jesus. She becomes more perfectly one in love and thus draws closer to the Day of the Lord.

THE DYNAMISM OF THE PRAYER AFTER COMMUNION

The Prayer after Communion often speaks of this growth of the Church. Every time the congregation disperses after being sanctified, beautified, and newly strengthened by the Eucharistic meal, it is capable of celebrating the Eucharist in a more perfect way the next time it meets. From Mass to Mass the Church advances toward the complete union, the perfect love, and the unshadowed joy of heaven.

In closing this chapter let us cite some Prayers after Communion prayers taken at random; they show how the liturgical mystery is the prefiguration and beginning of heavenly joy:

> "Lord, we are nourished by the bread of life you give us. May this mystery we now celebrate help us to reach eternal life with you" (Saturday after Ash Wednesday).
>
> "Lord, may your sacraments fully effect in us what they signify. Then we shall someday enter into perfect possession of the mystery we now celebrated in ritual form" (Thirtieth Sunday in Ordinary Time).
>
> "Lord, may your faithful have their sure foundation in your eternal gifts. As they receive them for food, may they ever desire them, and desiring without cease, be nourished by them for eternity" (Septuagesima, in the Roman Missal).

15.

Prayer for the Church and the World

THE MASS, A PRAYER FOR THE CHURCH
AND ALL MANKIND

The foregoing chapters have shown that at Mass we receive into ourselves the seed of our resurrection; that the Mass is oriented to the future and even to the last days (it is eschatological); and that the Prayers after Communion already turn our attention to heaven. But the Mass is still an earthly liturgy. We must not think of it as a mystical exercise, in the derogatory sense of the term, that is, an evasion of time and of the toils, cares, and troubles of the men of our day.

We are warned against such an interpretation, first of all, by the insistence with which the Church prays for peace at Mass. The petition occurs several times in the Roman Canon, and, at every Mass, becomes more pressing as Communion approaches. The Lord's Prayer calls for reconciliation between offender and offended. Immediately after it we pray: ". . . grant us peace in our day." The priest prays aloud for the peace and unity of the Church. He then addresses his desire to the people: "The peace of the

Lord be with you always." Finally he breaks the bread, an action which is a sign of unity and peace, and as he does so, the congregation sings a triple invocation to the Lamb of God, the last one concluding with "grant us peace."

What peace is meant here? To begin with, it is quite evidently the interior peace of each of us, our peace with God. What separates us from God and stirs his "anger" is sin. The Mass, however, is our sacrifice for the forgiveness of sins. That is why we so frequently ask God to accept our sacrifice, to let it please him. Moreover, the Mass invites us to offer ourselves, to immolate ourselves, not by indulging in self-destruction or masochism, but by renouncing everything that separates us from God or acts as an obstacle to our doing his will completely. Such obedience is the first condition of inner peace.

But this peace cannot remain locked up in ourselves. If we are at peace with God and ourselves, that can only be due to love. We will then be a source of peace and spread it to others around us. We will be among those "blessed . . . peacemakers [who] shall be called sons of God" (Matthew 5:9),[1] that is, the imitators and intimates of God.

Our peace will spread to those close to us and thereby to the Church, our Mother. The Mass prayers often seek peace and unity for the Church; these are the supreme blessings for any assembly, and they are the chief fruit of the Eucharist.[2] The prayer for peace is not at all restricted to interior peace for individuals and to quiet, undisturbed lives for members of the Church, it is an ardent missionary prayer embracing the whole world and indeed the whole universe.

What is the Church in essence, after all, if we look not to its divine origin (the three divine Persons from whom it emanates and whom it resembles), but to its material, that is, the men of whom it is formed? It is a real hodgepodge of created beings who differ from one another in race, nationality, social class, political and professional allegiance, culture, and even religious tendency. The Church gathers them all into Noah's ark or into the canvas which Peter in a vision saw being let down from heaven and in which were "all the earth's four-legged creatures and reptiles and birds of the sky" (Acts 10:12). The Church is not made up of people who are alike or already in harmony with each other, but of people who are distinctive, different, and divided. It is not easy to establish peace among them. When Jesus said: "My mission is to spread, not peace, but division" (Matthew 10:34), he was not renouncing his ideal of peace but voicing the truth that the establishment of true peace requires a spiritual violence, a renunciation, and a discipline of the appetites, egoisms, and sectarian tendencies that are only too natural to man.

The Church also has its lost children: those who have, inwardly or outwardly as well, left it though sin, abandonment of the faith, or rebellion. To pray for the peace and unity of the Church means praying that the lost sheep will be brought back and the ungrateful son found again. "In mercy and love unite all your children wherever they may be" (Third Eucharistic Prayer; cf. John 11:52). To pray for the peace and unity of the Church means praying for sinful Christians.

Finally, even if the Church were perfectly united and at peace, it is not a closed society, an independent body without concern for the world of men and temporal affairs. It is in the world as a leaven in dough; it is the sacrament, that is, the sign and cause, of salvation for all mankind.[3] When we pray for peace and unity, our prayer may know no limit except that set by the will of the God, who wants all men to be saved (1 Tim. 2:4), and by the desire of Christ, who intended his death to be redemptive for all sinners. In the Eucharist, as on the Cross, the blood of the new and everlasting covenant is shed for all.[4] Thus the Third Eucharistic Prayer says: "Advance the peace and salvation of all the world."

The missionary and universalist perspective as regards the salvation achieved by the Eucharist is brought out especially well in the Fourth Eucharistic Prayer:

> Even when he [man] disobeyed you and lost your friendship you did not abandon him to the power of death, but *helped all men* to seek and find you. . . . we offer you his body and blood, the acceptable sacrifice *which brings salvation to the whole world.* . . . Lord, remember those for whom we offer this sacrifice, especially N. our Pope, N. our bishop, and bishops and clergy everywhere. Remember those who take part in this offering, those here present and all your people [therefore the whole Church, with no exception at any level], and *all who seek you with a sincere heart.* Remember those who have died in the peace of Christ and *all the dead* whose faith is known to you alone.

The same Eucharistic Prayer ends by asking that we may "enter into our heavenly inheritance, in the company of the Virgin Mary, the Mother of God, and your apostles and saints. Then, in your kingdom, freed from the corruption of sin and death, we shall sing your glory *with every creature.*" The peace thus sought in the Eucharist in such a universalist way is not something abstract and timeless. It is a "peace in our day" (prayer after the Lord's Prayer).

It would evidently be a mockery for us simply to wish for peace within ourselves, in the Church, and throughout the world, and yet not work for the coming of peace. The beatitude in the Sermon on the Mount is addressed not to those who dream of peace but to those who *make* peace. To build peace means practicing justice and charity; it means fighting for justice and charity, and therefore struggling against injustice and lovelessness. It may rightly be said that the Church as such, like the Eucharist and the Mass, has nothing to do with politics or labor unions. But the men who make up the Church and who live by the Eucharist and really share in the Mass cannot regard themselves as dispensed from temporal involvement and from the fight to improve the lot of their fellowmen.

We must, then, take seriously and give concrete reference to the intercessions found in the Eucharistic Prayers. In the Roman Canon these intercessions are found both before and after the consecration; in the other Eucharistic Prayers they are all placed after the consecration. Why this is so we shall explain in the next chapter. But this manner of enveloping, or at least of being set alongside, the consecration shows that there is a close bond between the Eucharistic mystery and prayer for the world.

THE PRAYER OF THE FAITHFUL

We may legitimately feel that the wording of these intercessions is quite general and even "churchy," that is, conventional. This is because a liturgical prayer is composed for repetition over long periods and in very different circumstances and contexts. Such prayers cannot be worded so as to reflect events of the day, such as, for example, a serious strike, a war, or an earthquake.

But we can flesh out, particularize, and, so to speak, dramatize these very general petitions which occur during the Eucharist by use of a prayer that comes between the Liturgy of the Word and the Liturgy of the Eucharist. I am referring to the "general intercessions," which since the Council have come into renewed use in the Roman rite.[5]

The term "general" has a double reference. From the viewpoint of the authors of the intercessions, "general" means that they are to spring from the community of the baptized as a whole; no one is excluded but catechumens. This is why the official name for the general intercessions is "Prayer of the Faithful." "Faithful" here has its technical meaning: in order to pronounce this prayer, one must possess the baptismal priesthood shared by all who are fully members of the Church. This prayer is not in the strict sense a priestly or diaconal liturgy to which the people reply as they do, for example, to the greeting of the priest at the beginning of Mass or to the dialogue that opens the Preface. The Prayer of the Faithful is indeed introduced and concluded by the celebrant, but it belongs to the whole assembly of the baptized. The intentions may be spoken by a priest or deacon, but they may also be spoken by a layperson. In any event, the prayer, properly speaking, consists of invocations which all (including the priest, who is, after all, one of the baptized) ought to pray together.

The term "general" acquired its full meaning if we consider the objects for which we pray. In this respect the universality is unlimited, and in fact the petitions look to a great extent beyond the boundaries of the Church. In the regulations issued for the composition of the intercessions, four comprehensive categories are envisaged. Two of them are, we might say, "ecclesiastical": one includes the broad intentions of the Church, but we must remember that these are quite often missionary, ecumenical, even world-wide in nature. We know, for example, how dear to the Pope's heart is the cause of peace between nations. The fourth category — the second that is Church-oriented — concerns the community present at Mass. But this same community ought, of course, to be open and in vital communication with the life of local society and society at large.

The second category looks directly to temporal concerns: for those in authority; justice; elementary education; development. The third looks to all in need; here we can certainly pray for the spiritually needy, such as sinners and the dead. But let us not forget that it is a Christian act, and not simply a humanistic one, to pray for the hungry, the ill, the prisoners, the lonely, and the desperate.

This wide range of possibilities allows us to adapt the Prayer of the Faithful to the community present on a given day. The preoccupations and anxieties of our contemporaries and neighbors, the subjects being discussed on television, in the newspapers, and in the marketplace can enter into the Prayer of the Faithful and thus give the Mass a human dimension it would not have if we were content to use only pre-determined hieratic formulas. There is no question here of distorting, humanizing, or "demythologizing" the Eucharistic liturgy. The liturgy must preserve its biblical inspiration, its sober style, and its mystery. But in the minds and prayers of those who celebrate, the Eucharist cannot fail to be colored by, and focused upon, present reality by the living word of the homily and by the concrete petitions of the Prayer of the Faithful which comes just before the sacrifice.

Against this background the prayers for peace —
always peace! — will take on new depth and intensity
in the minds of all present.

[1]Cf. Luke 6:35, "Love your enemy and do good; lend without expecting repayment. Then will your recompense be great. You will rightly be called sons of the Most High."

[2]Cf. the Prayer over the Gifts for the feast of Corpus Christi.

[3]Cf. *Dogmatic Constitution on the Church*, nos. 1, 9, 48; *Constitution on the Sacred Liturgy*, no. 5 *Pastoral Constitution on the Church in the Modern World*, nos. 42, 45.

[4]The text says "for many," "for the multitude," but these phrases are Semitisms and imply no limitation.

[5]Cf. *Constitution on the Sacred Liturgy*, no. 53.

16.

Adoration in Spirit and in Truth

The first apologists for Christianity claimed that Christians had neither temple nor altar. This should not lead us to conclude that the Christian religion is wholly interior and has no place for a liturgical cultus. That kind of spiritualism would verge on laicism.

The point was, rather, that pagans saw in their temple the dwelling place of a god, and their worship was closely linked to sacred places such as woods or springs. The Jewish liturgy similarly could be celebrated only at Jerusalem, so that during the Exile (cf. Dan. 3:38), and again after the Holy City was sacked by Titus, the sacrifices came to an end. The Christian sacrifice, on the contrary, was the fulfillment of Malachi's prophecy: "From the rising of the sun, even to its setting, . . . everywhere they bring sacrifice to my name" (Mal. 1:11). The Christian temple is the "church," that is, the *ekklēsia* or "convoked assembly" of the faithful who in their own person are "the house of God" (cf. 1 Cor. 3:16, 2 Cor. 6:16; Eph. 2:19, 1 Peter 2:5). There need only be "two or three gathered in [his] name" for Christ to be in their midst.

The offerings made in the Christian sacrifice are

no longer goats or bullocks; there is no more bloodshed nor sizzling fat, the smoke of which "rises as an
acceptable odor." Now there are only "spiritual
sacrifices," a "eucharist," a thanksgiving, and a
Church which offers itself. The heart of sacrifice is
not the gift but the intention or spirit which motivates
the gift.[1]

TRUTH: THE REALISM OF THE LITURGY

Nonetheless, Christianity does have a liturgy; it
has church buildings, stone altars, offerings taken
from created things. Moreover, it is Christ himself
who offers himself; the Word incarnate, the Head of
mankind and First-born of all creation, immolates
himself in genuine sacrifice. The food he bestows is his
flesh, which he delivered up for the life of the world.
His blood is shed for the forgiveness of sins. And this
sacrifice is not simply a pious allegory for our
instruction; it is a sacrifice "in truth."

The Christian, then, must betake himself to this
sacrifice in which the work of his salvation is both
commemorated and brought about. He is called to the
church where, at least every Sunday or "Lord's day,"
he will enter into communion with the Church and
take part in the visible sacrifice of his Savior. His faith
is not simply a pack of concepts, an ideal construction,
or an evocation of memories that are constantly
growing dim. His faith takes flesh in visible gestures
and sounding words. It finds support in realities as
solid as the stone of the altar; it sustains itself with
realities as nourishing as bread and wine, and as warm
and alive as the flesh and blood of Christ.

SPIRIT: THE ROLE OF THE HOLY SPIRIT

This worship "in truth" is also a worship "in spirit," for the material things we have mentioned are signs. Even the body of Christ in its substantial or physical reality is a sign of that Body which is his Church. The latter in turn is both visible and invisible, being composed of many members united by love, in whom God will be all in all at the end of time.

Worship "in spirit" also means worship "in the Holy Spirit." The Spirit plays a part in the Eucharist of which Latin Christians are too often unaware. If we understand that role of the Spirit, we will be protected against thinking of the Mass and sacraments as though they were mechanical.

THE INVOCATION OF THE HOLY SPIRIT, OR EPICLESIS

While the human priest physically pronounces the words, it is these words of Christ, assigned to the priest to speak, which transform the bread and wine into Christ's body and blood. The priest, therefore, does not speak to them as though he himself were the source of their power. Furthermore, the consecration is framed in the Eucharistic Prayer; it is part of a whole made up of humble entreaty and invocation. The Greek word corresponding to the Latin *invocatio* is *epiclēsis.* It occurs in the Eastern liturgies and designates the invocation in which the celebrant calls upon the Holy Spirit to effect the consecration which the words of Christ effected at the Last Supper.

The Roman Canon (First Eucharistic Prayer) contains no epiclesis in this strict sense. As a result of this, and also of absurd situations conjured up by some Latin casuists,[2] some Eastern polemicists have reproached the Roman Church for the lack of an authentic religious sense in its liturgy. In answer, we must point out that although the Holy Spirit is not expressly mentioned in the Roman Canon, there are nonetheless two prayers which have approximately the function of an epiclesis. The first occurs immediately before the consecration and asks God to effect it: "Bless and approve our offering; make it acceptable to you, an offering in spirit and in truth. Let it become for us the body and blood of Jesus Christ, your only Son, our Lord."

After the anamnesis and its continuation in the recall of the sacrifices of Abel, Abraham, and Melchisedech, the Roman Canon, using figurative but rather obscure language (the transfer of the sacrifice to the heavenly altar by an angel), petitions that the mystery be brought to fulfillment.

The new Eucharistic Prayers recently introduced into the Roman liturgy all have two epicleses in the strict sense of the term, that is, invocations calling for the intervention of the Holy Spirit. These occur just before the words of consecration are pronounced and just after the anamnesis. The first asks the Holy Spirit to bring about the consecration: "Let your Spirit come upon these gifts to make them holy, *so that they may become for us the body and blood of our Lord, Jesus Christ*" (Second Eucharistic Prayer). We have underlined those words which are quite similar to words in the corresponding prayer of the Roman Canon. We find them again in the pre-consecratory epiclesis of the Third and Fourth Eucharistic Prayers. They express the conviction of all the early Fathers, as summed by St. John Damascene: "The change of bread into Christ's body takes place by the power of the Holy Spirit."[3]

The epiclesis which occurs after the anamnesis

petitions not the consecration but a fruitful communion; that is, it asks for the love and unity which sharing in the Eucharistic bread should bring with it: "May all of us who share in the body and blood of Christ be brought together in unity by the Holy Spirit" (Second Eucharistic Prayer). The same petition occurs in the other two Eucharistic Prayers, but the latter make explicit the ultimate purpose of this unity and of the institution of the Eucharist. Thus the petition in the Fourth Prayer reads: "By your Holy Spirit, gather all who share this bread and wine into the one body of Christ, *a living sacrifice of praise."*

It is easy to see why the Church should attribute this ultimate effect of the Eucharist to the Holy Spirit. He is love, he is gift, he is the bond between the Father and the Son. He is the wellspring of charity; he is the soul of the Church — of its rich inner life, its fraternal "communion," and its missionary dynamism. In the Nicene Creed, as in the Apostles' Creed, both of which have a Trinitarian structure, after expressing our faith in God the Father and Creator and in Jesus the Redeemer, we also profess our faith in the Spirit who sanctifies. The articles which follow upon the mention of the third Person are not thrown in haphazardly. They name the works which are proper to the Spirit of love: the one, holy, catholic, and apostolic Church that was born on Pentecost; the communion of saints and the sharing in holy things, especially the wealth contained in the sacraments[4]; baptism, which brings forgiveness of sins, because it is the Spirit who sanctifies the water of baptism and because, being love, he is himself the forgiveness of sins; finally it is he who will raise us to new life at the end of time and introduce us to the life of the world that is coming.

Now we can understand why, in these three new

Eucharistic Prayers, the intercessions are placed not only after the consecration and anamnesis but also after the epiclesis. We pray for the peace of the Church and the world, with all that such peace implies; for the unity and growth of the people of God; for the salvation of sinners; for the entry of the dead into the full light of God. All these, however, flow indeed from the Eucharist, but they do so as the work of the Holy Spirit.

The Mass is not restricted to making the immolated Christ present on the altar nor even to offering him. Rather, it must influence the whole life of the Church, its whole work of unifying and sanctifying. So, too, each of us must not only offer the immolated Christ but also ourselves with him, and thus become a living sacrifice for the praise of the Father's glory. A ritual sacrifice is not enough; it must be completed by a spiritual sacrifice, that is, a sacrifice offered by the power of the Holy Spirit.

Our adoration is adoration in truth (the sacramental realism of the Eucharist), but it attains its full truth only if it is also an adoration in spirit and in the Spirit.

IT IS NOT ENOUGH TO "GO TO MASS"

A Catholic is a person who "goes to Mass." Otherwise he is not a Catholic. That by itself, however, is not enough to make him a Catholic. The Mass is not a weekly religious act that dispenses a person from all other obligations; it is, on the contrary, a summit toward which his whole daily life tends and from which it descends once again. It is the heart to which and from which everything flows. It is the home and hearth where all are nourished and find warmth.

The purpose, then, of our attempt to introduce the reader of these pages to the mystery of the Mass is not simply that he may know what he is about when he attends Mass. It is not simply to give him "ideas" about the Mass. The purpose is that he may come to live by the Mass. The holy sacrifice will not be *his* sacrifice unless it becomes the focus of all his efforts to evangelize himself and others; unless he derives from it the strength he needs for his daily tasks; unless he makes of it a Eucharist for all the gifts he has received — unless, that is, he makes of it a thanksgiving "for everything" (Eph. 5:20; 1 Thess. 1:2; 5:18), since "everything is a gift."

The Mass should not be a cultic intermission in a person's spiritual life. The spiritual life has its proper truth only if it derives its nourishment from this act of worship, and finds in it the language with which to express itself outwardly and socially. Our efforts to love, if they are not to degenerate into philanthropy and sentimentalism, must draw inspiration from "the first and irreplaceable wellspring of the Christian spirit" (Pope Pius X), which is active participation in liturgical worship. When St. Paul urges his brothers "through the mercy of God to offer your bodies as a living sacrifice holy and acceptable to God, your spiritual worship" (Rom. 12:1), and when St. Peter exhorts them to be "living stones, built as an edifice of spirit, into a holy priesthood, offering spiritual sacrifices acceptable to God through Jesus Christ" (1 Peter 2:5), neither apostle is thinking that good behavior or a life of brotherhood or the effort to christianize the world is, by itself, an acceptable worship. Neither, on the other hand, do they think that liturgical worship is enough to save men and glorify God if it is not prolonged in a "spiritual worship" in which each individual makes the sacrifice of Christ his own and extends it to his own, according to the requirements and graces of his state.

It would be a grave error not to put the sacrifice of Christ at the heart of Catholicism. It would be liturgicism to think that everything needful has been done once Mass is celebrated and that the community is dissolved and freed of any further commitment when the celebrant tells them: "Go in the peace of Christ."

I pray that this little book may help us realize that the Mass is not to be reverently wrapped in a cloth and buried in a hole in the ground. The talent here given us must bring forth fruit, so that when the Master returns he may receive back his gift with interest. True adorers must adore the Father in truth (John 4:23-24), but since God is spirit, they must also be adorers in spirit.

---

[1]Cf. Joseph A. Jungmann, S. J., *The Mass of the Roman Rite: Its Origins and Development (Missarum Solemnia)*, tr. by Francis A. Brunner, C.SS.R. (New York: Benziger), I (1951), pp. 22–28, 186; revised and abridged edition in one volume, tr. by Francis A. Brunner, C.SS.R., revised by Charles K. Riepe (1959), pp. 13–18, 140–141.

[2]I am thinking especially of the hypothetical case in which a priest would pronounce the words of consecration over all the loaves in a bakery or all the vats in a wine-cellar. No theologian today would admit the efficacy of such a "formula" stripped of any liturgical context; it would manifestly be cut off from any intention of the Church, that is, from that intention which the celebrant must make his own in administering any sacrament whatever.

[3]St. John Damascene, *The Orthodox Faith*, IV, 13.

[4]*Communio sanctorum* has a different meaning depending on whether we take *sanctorum* as the genitive of *sancti* ("the saints") or of *sancta* ("holy things").

REVIEW QUESTIONS

Chapter 1, pages 1-12

1. What is the most obvious and immediate feature of the Mass? Give some citations from early Christianity which mention this feature.
2. The author says that the assembly of the faithful for Mass is a "mystery." What does he mean?
3. Several times during Mass the celebrant greets the faithful with the words "The Lord be with you." What other words would be appropriate to greet the people at Mass and why?
4. What makes the Christian assembly holy and worthy of respect?
5. Can you think of any ceremonies or gestures within the Mass that remind one of baptism? What connection is there between baptism and the Mass?
6. List the various rules needed to celebrate the Eucharist. What is the function of each?
7. How does a congregation show its unity and vitality? How did the early Church achieve order and unity at the celebration of the Eucharist?
8. What is meant by "concelebration"? When is concelebration required? Why?

Chapter 2, pages 13-22

9. What is so important about congregational singing at Mass?
10. The Mass re-presents the sacrifice of the Cross. What does the author mean when he says that "the Cross is not simply and solely a redemptive sacrifice"?
11. How do we relate the ideas of the Cross and the Supper in referring to the Mass?
12. What is the meaning of "eucharist"? How does this definition apply to the Mass?

13. What is meant by the term "Liturgy of the Word"? What elements of praise are to be found in it?

14. How would you answer someone who asks: "What sacrifice or immolation is there in a series of songs and readings?"

Chapter 3, pages 23-32

15. What does the term "Liturgy of the Eucharist" refer to? Give as many names for the Mass as you know.

16. What is the purpose of the Preface in the Mass?

17. To "give thanks" is a very profound idea as applied to the Mass. Can you elaborate on this statement?

18. The Mass has been called "a perfect act of thanksgiving." How is this so?

19. Discuss the meaning of the word *Amen*. What is the "great Amen" of the Mass? Why is this "Amen" so significant?

20. What meaning can be attributed to the "Amen" which the communicant says after the priest says "The body of Christ"?

Chapter 4, pages 33-38

21. What ideas are contained in the word "offering"? When does the offering of the Mass end?

22. How many "elevations" occur during the Mass? When do they take place?

23. What do the faithful offer at Mass?

Chapter 5, pages 39-48

24. The Mass has been called an exchange of gifts between God and man. What are God's gifts to men? What are men's gifts to God?

25. What value does the "collection" have at Mass besides providing money for the parish's needs?

26. In prayer we often ask God for this or that temporal favor. What does *authentic* prayer ask for?

27. In what way is the Mass a "school of perfect prayer"?

Chapter 6, pages 49-55

28. Give your definition of "the Church." What is the relationship between the Eucharist and the Church?
29. Why is it important that the Mass be celebrated in community and not simply as an individual act?
30. In earlier days the kiss of peace was given before Communion. Our new rite for Mass allows for a handshake or some other sign of peace at this time. Do you approve of this practice? Why or why not?
31. In many cases the Mass is simply a dead ceremony. What must we do to make it a dynamic force in our lives?

Chapter 7, pages 56-61

32. What do you think is the greatest hindrance to loving God?
33. What would you advise a person who says he feels no emotion in receiving our Lord in Communion?

Chapter 8, pages 62-67

34. Why is it necessary to celebrate the Eucharist every day? Use an example from the Bible to help in answering this question.
35. Why is bread such a fitting material for our sacramental offering?

Chapter 9, pages 68-75

36. What symbolism is attached to the wine used at Mass?
37. The wine is offered and consecrated in a cup. What meaning is attached to the cup?
38. Does receiving Communion under both forms add any special graces? What value is there in drinking from the chalice?

Chapter 10, pages 76-86

39. The Mass is considered both a meal and a sacrifice.
    Discuss the true meaning of "sacrifice."
40. The Mass is said to reproduce the Last Supper. How can
    the Last Supper be considered a sacrifice?
41. What does it mean to say that the Mass is "sacra-
    mental"?
42. What effects should the Mass have on our daily lives?

Chapter 11, pages 87-91

43. If the Mass re-presents Christ's death on the cross,
    what consideration is given to his resurrection and the
    other mysteries of his life?

Chapter 12, pages 92-96

44. Explain this statement at the beginning of Chapter 12:
    "The Eucharist gives eternal life."
45. Holy anointing used to be considered the sacrament of
    the dying. What perspective did the Second Vatican
    Council give to this sacrament?
46. What is the meaning of "Viaticum"? What is its
    purpose?
47. What should be our criterion in receiving the holy
    Eucharist?

Chapter 13, pages 97-105

48. What is the difference between the "Day of the Lord" as
    used in the Old Testament and its meaning in the New
    Testament?
49. We say that the consecration effects the "real presence"
    of Christ. What does this term mean?
50. Define "anamnesis." What are the three principal
    mysteries mentioned in the anamnesis? How does each
    of these mysteries contain the future?
51. What do we mean by the "parousia"? Is it included in the
    anamnesis in any way?

52. What link is there between the Old Testament sacrifices of Abel, Abraham, and Melchizedek and our Eucharistic sacrifice?

53. Explain the paradoxical title "memorial of the future" as applied to the Mass.

Chapter 14, pages 106-112

54. Why is baptism conferred only once but the Eucharist is repeated again and again?

55. Describe the ancient vigil service as observed by the early Christians. Why was the Eucharist celebrated on Sunday?

56. What is meant by the "annual Passover"? What is the relationship between the various seasons and feasts of the liturgical year and the Eucharist?

57. Why are the feasts of the liturgical seasons observed year after year? Are they not simply commemorations of past events — the birth of Jesus, his baptism, resurrection, ascension, etc.?

58. Do you agree with this statement: "Advent is a time to prepare our souls for Christmas"? Explain your answer.

Chapter 15, pages 113-120

59. Give some instances in which peace is prayed for in the Mass. What is this "peace" which we pray for? Why do we pray so insistently for it in the Mass?

60. Can you give another name for the "general intercessions"? What meanings does the word "general" have here?

61. List the four categories which the general intercessions should ideally fit into. Explain each category briefly.

Chapter 16, pages 121-128

62. Why does the Church command that we participate in the Eucharistic sacrifice at least once a week, on Sunday?

63. Define the word "epiclesis." With your missalette in hand, locate the epicleses in the four Eucharistic Prayers.

64. What exactly is the role of the Holy Spirit in the Mass?

65. A Catholic is often identified as one who "goes to Mass." Would you raise any objections to this definition?